The Lover of God

Rabindranath Tagore

The Lover of God

RABINDRANATH TAGORE

Translated by
Tony K. Stewart &
Chase Twichell

Copper Canyon Press
A Kage-an Book

Printed in the United States of America

ACKNOWLEDGMENTS

These poems have appeared in the following publications. We are grateful to their editors: *Brick* (Canada), *Columbia Journal, The Drunken Boat, The Electronic Poetry Review.*

Cover art: Untitled Kalighat painting, V&A Picture Library

Frontispiece: Signed photograph of Rabindranath Tagore, c. 1920, private collection of Tony K. Stewart

Copper Canyon Press is in residence under the auspices of the Centrum Foundation at Fort Worden State Park in Port Townsend, Washington. Centrum sponsors artist residencies, education workshops for Washington State students and teachers, Blues, Jazz, and Fiddle Tunes festivals, classical music performances, and the Port Townsend Writers' Conference.

LIBRARY OF CONGRESS CATALOGING-IN-PUBLICATION DATA

Tagore, Rabindranath, 1861–1941.
The Lover of God / Rabindranath Tagore; translated by Tony K. Stewart and Chase Twichell.
p. cm.
"Kage-an book."
In English and Bengali.
ISBN 1-55659-196-9 (alk. paper)
1. Religious poetry, Bengali—Translations into English. I. Stewart, Tony Kevin. II. Twichell, Chase, 1950– III. Title.
PK1723.I68 2003
891.4'414—DC22

2003016475

98765432
FIRST PRINTING

Kage-an Books (from the Japanese, meaning "Shadow Hermitage" and representing the "shadow work" of the translator) presents the world's great poetic traditions, ancient and modern, in vivid translations under the editorship of Sam Hamill.

COPPER CANYON PRESS
Post Office Box 271
Port Townsend, Washington 98368
www.coppercanyonpress.org

Contents

The Lover of God

Introduction

Sometime late in 1875, the prominent Calcutta journal of Bengali arts and letters *Bhāratī* published the first of eight poems by a newly discovered seventeenth-century Vaiṣṇava religious poet, Bhānusiṃha, or Sun Lion. That journal would eventually publish thirteen over the next six years. The poems told of the love of Lord Kṛṣṇa, through the ministrations of a friend to Kṛṣṇa's adolescent lover, Rādhā. Typical of the genre, the confidante was an older woman—the poet's persona—who chides and scolds Kṛṣṇa, soothes Rādhā's anguish, and ruefully comments on the plight of all who suffer the love of this fickle master. Typical, too, was the language, Brajabuli, a long-dead literary dialect of Bengali reserved for the exclusive use of Vaiṣṇava poets. At the time, it was a notable discovery as scholars within the academy were at pains to construct a proper literary history for India, one of the earliest nation-building exercises in the political and intellectual ferment that was late-nineteenth-century Calcutta. Yet several years would pass before leading critics discovered that they had been drawn into a somewhat embarrassing scenario: Bhānusiṃha did not really exist. And perhaps even worse, the true author was none other than a precocious fourteen-year-old boy poet named Rabindranath Tagore.

So began one of the most curious literary episodes of the period of nationalist India, a mild exposé that alleged deceit, fraud, and, worst of all, gullibility. At the time of this discovery, Rabindranath was beginning to distinguish himself from his enormously talented siblings, some of whom were probably privy to the ruse that originated in this family-sponsored journal. His poetry and his prose were beginning to draw considerable attention, yet as his fame increased he would never abandon these first poems, just as he would for years refuse to acknowledge having written them, as if he wanted them to be neither closely examined nor ignored. He would throw up obstacles at every turn, but would tease his audience by drawing attention to the songs and just as quickly deflect any serious discussion of them. In 1884 he published a fictional biography of Bhānusiṃha, mocking scholars with its sarcasm and wit, but dropping tantalizing clues to Bhānusiṃha's real identity, tacitly acknowledging that Bhānusiṃha was he (see Appendix). He would continue to criticize the "author" of the poems, as well as those scholars who might try alternately to beatify or to denigrate the poet, this game of cat and mouse continuing as he added more poems to the sequence. Today many schoolchildren know these songs by heart and delight in their recitation.

Much of the pleasure of these poems derives from their adaptation of an overtly religious form well-known to any Bengali speaker: the celebration of the love of Kṛṣṇa and Rādhā. Inspiration came from the Bengali god-man of the sixteenth century, Kṛṣṇa Caitanya (1486–1533); his followers — called Vaiṣṇavas for their devotion to a particular form of Lord Viṣṇu, Kṛṣṇa — developed a distinctive lyric style in a language reserved exclusively for this praise. Today more than eight thousand of these poems circulate.[1] These Vaiṣṇava poets sang the exploits of Lord Kṛṣṇa as he played with his friends, the cowherd boys of the idyllic land of Braj, but they sang most delightedly of Kṛṣṇa's discovery of adolescent love. His protracted affairs with the young cowherd maidens, the *gopīs*, have been a favorite topic in Bengal certainly as far back as the twelfth-century Sanskrit *Gīta Govinda* of Jayadeva and the slightly later Bengali *Śrī Kṛṣṇa Kīrtana* of Caṇḍīdāsa. Tagore's poems name Rādhā as Kṛṣṇa's favorite, as is hinted at in the scriptural tenth book of the Sanskrit *Bhāgavata Purāṇa*. Her love for him is selfless and unselfconscious; her lack of self-interest drives Kṛṣṇa to distraction. She innocently deploys all of the coquettishness and trickery at the disposal of a woman bent on attracting a man; her artifices provide a catalog of amorous technique. Perhaps

1. For the best translations of this poetry, see *In Praise of Krishna: Songs from the Bengali*, trans. Edward C. Dimock Jr. and Denise Levertov, with an introduction by Edward C. Dimock Jr. (Garden City, N.Y.: Anchor Books, Doubleday, 1967; reprint: Chicago: The University of Chicago Press, 1981).

most alluring is the unpredictable nature of her love, characterized as her *bāmatā,* or crooked temperament. Even God-as-Kṛṣṇa is captivated and so he pursues her in contrived encounters.

In one popular episode Kṛṣṇa poses as a toll collector who waylays Rādhā until she bargains her way free. In another he disguises himself as a ferryman, stopping midstream to extract his fare from the penniless, but hardly helpless, Rādhā. Once he followed Rādhā and the other *gopīs* to the river and stole their clothes while they were bathing; one by one they have to emerge from the water and present themselves to him before being allowed to leave. Perhaps the most celebrated episode is the famous round dance, where the *gopīs* slip out to meet Kṛṣṇa on a brooding monsoon night; such is their passion this night that he multiplies himself to dance simultaneously with all who gathered. But mostly the songs are about trysts, or, more poignantly, the missed assignation and the longing for union. Rādhā and the *gopīs* burn in the fires of separation, a pain called *viraha.* That exquisite pain is intensified by the sound of Kṛṣṇa's flute, Muralī, or its echo in the plaintive cry of the *bihaṅga* bird, or by any of a myriad of other reminders. *Viraha* becomes the dominant trope for Bengali Vaiṣṇava poetry, so naturally it is the dominant mood of Rabindranath's Vaiṣṇava songs. In these songs he inhabits the persona of an experienced confidante, named Bhānu, bent on consoling an unconsolable Rādhā. But in a twist, the focus sometimes shifts *to* Bhānu, and there we see Rabindranath's distinctive voice, expressing concerns about mortality and divinity that belie the Vaiṣṇava form of these poems.

And so this small batch of poetry that began its printed life anonymously, after a short period in the spotlight reentered the sphere of the unread, its author publicly distanced from its production, the interest of the poetry reader and critic reduced to distracted curiosity. Yet the poems are filled with a power and poignancy, an immediacy and presence that readers have come to expect from one of the world's greatest poets. Over the course of some sixty-five years Tagore could not leave alone these poems, a private world of whose importance to him we can only speculate.

On Translating Bhānu

We have rendered these poems into English in the spirit and tone of the revisions finished shortly before Tagore died. As will become apparent—and true to Rabindranath's own experimentation with the poems—we opted to capture the mood and emotion as much as the literal content. The impulse behind the decision was based in part on the checkered reception and interpretation of the poems themselves and our attempts to negotiate the often boggling array of subterfuges adopted to disguise his voice, a strategy that lent anonymity and distance to the poems' overt religious connotations.

The choice to translate these poems was easy enough, for any poetry that occupies such a gifted author for the better part of seven decades has earned a lasting readership. How these translations came about is nearly as convoluted as the history of the poems themselves. In 1978, when I was studying Bengali in the intensive program run by the American Institute of Indian Studies in Calcutta, I first read these poems as an extension of my work on old Vaiṣṇava literature. Appropriately, my initiation came through the perspective of a woman, my Bengali teacher Ms. Supriya Chatterjee, who at considerable risk to her own modesty afforded me insights that would have remained opaque to a nonnative male speaker of the language. I picked up the translations a few years later, gratefully reading them in tutorials with Clinton B. Seely and the late Edward C. Dimock at The University of Chicago. Their insights have, over the years, deepened my own. As a new student of the language, I struggled to reconstruct the etymological roots of obscure terms, more than a few of which defy the comprehensive dictionaries available for Bengali—Rabindranath loved etymologies and the playful double entendres they could engender in the malleable lexicon of Brajabuli. Still very much learning the language, I strove to master the idiosyncracies of Rabindranath's Brajabuli syntax, a feature of the poetry that is liable to confound the unwary. Then I set the project aside, stymied by the realization that these seemingly insignificant poems were anything but, yet unable to bring out what I intuited of their secrets. From time to time over the next twenty-odd years, I would reinitiate myself into these little poems and, with each new reading, marvel at their depth—their idiom of course now having become intimately familiar in my years of reading and translating Bengali. Each new encounter convinced me that they not only needed to be translated for the general reading public, but required a deft hand that exceeded any of my own aspirations as poet. I followed the inspired suggestion of poet and friend Lee Upton, which led me to Chase Twichell. As I mulled over the strategies for collaboration while working at the British Library in 1996, I translated for the third time all twenty-two songs, this time adding word-for-word breakdowns to be used as guides.

I approached Chase—we had not previously met, though I knew her poetry—and she agreed to look. For the next three years she looked, listened, and read Tagore, undertaking a personal yogic *sādhanā* (striving) not unlike that of the old Vaiṣṇava poets themselves. She took my literal translations of the Brajabuli and fired them into new poetry in English. In that sense, they are no longer Rabindranath's poems; they have become something new through my role as mediator or midwife and hers as poet-alchemist. Chase knows no Bengali or Brajabuli, and for that we are both grateful because it freed us from the constraints that plague most translators: the poems had to become hers in order to live—unlike me, she was not shackled by their original forms. Charmed by Rabindranath's precocity and cheekiness, mesmerized by the intricacies of Vaiṣṇava aesthetics, she has rendered that which is most likely to cross barriers of language and culture: the songs' intense emotion, Rādhā's thrill, her anguish, her exasperation, and her confidante's consoling. Even if Tagore was right that the conditions of their composition and his own proclivities made it impossible to judge the devotional mood of these poems as authentic to Vaiṣṇava standards, the Vaiṣṇava poets would still approve, I think, not only of the end product but of the process that rendered the emotions intelligible.

Ours was initially a strange endeavor that resulted in a true collaboration. I followed the Bengali dictum that later versions of texts are better than the mythical urtext (rejecting the decidedly Western fixation on the original), because the text once used takes a shape that reflects the interests and values of its users; earlier versions capture a historical moment, but the last versions demonstrate what endured and, therefore, was for their creator significant. The poems come from Rabindranath's last revisions.

The process was a laborious one, and for the curious who might like to peek at the process, let us look at the first twelve lines of song 3. I rained down upon Chase a torrent of renditions, starting with transliterations in roman script so that she could hear the music. This is what she first saw.

hṛdayaka sādha miśāola hṛdaye,
        kaṇṭhe vimalina mālā.
virahabiṣe dahi bahi gala rayanī,
        nahi nahi āola kālā.
bujhanu bujhanu sakhi viphala viphala saba,
        viphala e pīriti lehā —
viphala re e majhu jīvana yauvana,
        viphala re e majhu dehā!
cala sakhi gṛha cala, muñca nayana-jala,
        cala sakhi cala gṛhakāje,
mālati-mālā rākhaha bālā,
        chi chi sakhi maru maru lāje.

This transliteration was coupled with a word-for-word reading that retained the Brajabuli syntax and included notes on odd grammatical forms, nuances of tone, syntactical variations that included logical inferences quite alien to English grammar, and expositions on erotic symbolism sufficient to satisfy all but the most demanding of pedants. The technique is one that my old teacher and friend A. K. Ramanujan first taught me when we read several of these together in Chicago in the early eighties. Chase dubbed these "word clouds," the pathway into the poems. Here again the first twelve lines of song 3:

heart's / yearning, striving, worship / has been mixed, mingled / in heart /
on or around neck / devoid of stain, unsoiled / garland /.
pain of separation / with poison / bearing, enduring / melted, pass through, be overwhelmed / through or in night /,
not / not (= but [he] never) / came / Dark One (= Kṛṣṇa) /.
I understood, realized / I understood (~truly, surely) / friend, companion (f., voc.) / fruitless, lit. devoid of fruit or barren / fruitless / everything, all /,
Barren, fruitless / this / amorous love (~illicit) / passion (glossed as *anurāga*, "following after passion") —
Barren, fruitless / O (~yes; voc. after reduplication = affirmation)/ this / of me, my / life / youth, adolescence /,
barren, fruitless / O (~yes)/ this / of me, my / body /!

(N.B., the next four lines are [the author as] Bhānu consoling woman; but this is very un-Vaiṣṇava-like to have the author appear anywhere but in the signature line [*bhaṇitā*] at the end.)
Go, be off; or Let us be off (impv.) / dear friend, companion (f., voc.)/ home, house / go, be off (impv.) / wipe away, cleanse (impv.)/ eye- / water, tears /,
Go, be off; let us go (impv.) / dear friend, companion (f., voc.) / go, be off; let us go (impv.) / house, domestic / to work, to chores /,
jasmine / garland, flower necklace / save, keep / young girl (dim.) /,
chi-chi (a sound expressing exasperation, mild censure, sympathy;

somewhat like *tsk tsk*) / dear friend, companion (f., voc.) / (you) dying / dying (~you must just be dying) / of or with or from shame, humiliation, embarrassment /.

With this impression of the poem taking shape, the slavishly literal and unpoetic line-by-line translation followed; occasionally there would be two versions, one more literal than the other. Again the first twelve lines of song 3:

The desire of hearts he has joined in mine,
on my neck hangs garland unstained,
afire with parted love's poison
the night passed—the Dark One never came.
I understand, friend, all was fruitless.
Fruitless this passionate love,
yes, fruitless my life and youth,
fruitless this my body.
    Go, friend, go home, wipe away those tears.
    Go, friend, go do your chores,
    save your jasmine garland, young girl.
    How you must be dying from shame.

Chase then transformed these impressions, images, and ideas into a new poem:

He never came to me.
In the whole long dark he never came
to tend my lacerated heart.
I'm a girl with nothing, a tree
with neither flowers nor fruit.
    Go home, poor tragedy. Distract yourself
    with chores, dry your eyes. Go on now,
    dear tattered garland, limp with shame.

We are at a loss for words to describe precisely what these new poems are—except *poems;* clear, simple translations they cannot be—renderings perhaps, or re-creations. They are faithful, but not literal. The Bengali and the English do not match line for line. Rabindranath himself often voiced his frustration at the impossibility of capturing his Bengali world in English and so chose to eliminate much of what was culturally specific. But these poems are deeply rooted in Indian mythology and must be encountered on their own terms; their beauty and power lie in the physical and emotional landscape, and so we have invited the reader to enter that world, rather than change it. As for the strict forms in which the original poems were written, it seemed an empty exercise to force English into those particular strictures, which in the Bengali literary tradition are richly associative but which in English are not. The familiar fourteen-syllable *payār* couplet with its *aa bb cc* rhymes and the more intricate three-footed *tripadi* of variable length and rhyme were the first casualties of the process. And those familiar with the famous line in song 13, the onomatopoetic *ghana ghana rim jhim rim jhim rim jhim,* will undoubtedly be disappointed to discover that it is not there. In Brajabuli it mimics successfully the rhythmic sounds of monsoon rains and the ponderous roll of thunder, but to our ears it proves distracting in English. Choosing neither to leave it untranslated nor to render it into the nursery-rhyme pitter-patter of raindrops, Chase invokes the rain through imagery rather than sound. That and similar decisions will be evident to the Bengali speaker.

Throughout these poems, Rabindranath shows a fondness for other forms that diverge from English sensibilities, for instance the extensive use of vocatives, such as *sajani,* which means "best friend" (f.) or "companion" (f.), with overtones of confidante or helper; and *go,* which means "dear one" or "beloved." He also uses numerous particles of interjection—e.g., *re* or *he,* which can be translated as "O" or "hey," or simply as a mark of exclamation ("!")—that serve to punctuate a point or lend emotional force. When used indiscriminately by lesser poets, they are seen as fillers, but in his case they generally serve to bind together lines as a kind of refrain and add a musical quality that is difficult to replicate. Having already abandoned the formal structures that make these vocatives and particles useful in Brajabuli or Bengali, and finding no workable analogues in English, we often had to jettison those and other unique features of the language. But there was an added challenge: to publish without notes. Our goal was to make the poems accessible on their own terms; the inclusion of extensive notes signals a translator's defeat. Except for occasional names of unfamiliar flora and fauna (whose Latin designations would help few readers), everything in these poems should be somehow familiar.

One of the challenges of translation is the weighing of one faithfulness against another. In a sense it's the art of unfaithfulness. As Chase has put it, rather than building the houses and then trying to persuade Rādhā, Kṛṣṇa, and Bhānu to come live in them, she entered each poem by coming to her own terms with its voice, imagery, and emotional texture, while keeping in mind the dramatic arc of the entire sequence. For Bengali readers, we have included the original Brajabuli so that you might see for yourself where and how we have departed from the original and, perhaps more importantly, where we have captured the emotional force.

Our special thanks go to Clinton B. Seely, who not only set the text, but personally designed the elegant Bengali typeface, including creating additional conjunct consonants to meet my demand for a look that was traditional to Tagore's era. The editorial and production team at Copper Canyon Press—managing editor Michael Wiegers, production manager Amy Schaus Murphy, and copy editor David Caligiuri—are to be lauded for the brave way they initiated themselves into the Bengali script and transliteration schemes alien to any they had previously used. This little book's elegance is a tribute to their rare patience—and to the vision of Sam Hamill, who encouraged us to plunge ahead.

The sequence of the poems follows that of the final published versions, and it parallels the trajectory of Rādhā's experience, the devotee's experience, and the aging of both actors in the drama.

But we have retained the two uncollected poems (21, 22) that serve as coda and commentary to the body of the text. In retrospect, it is both amusing and perhaps not too far-fetched to see how in this long process we have embraced the roles of those we portray—Chase suffering the white heat of inspiration for an elusive spiritual goal only she could know, while I, having led her into this jungle, can but extend quiet company and a commiserating hand.

Tony K. Stewart
Raleigh, North Carolina
18 May 2003

The Poems of Sun Lion

১

বসন্ত আওল রে!
মধুকর গুন গুন, অমুয়া মঞ্জরী
কানন ছাওল রে।
শুন শুন সজনী হৃদয় প্রাণ মম
হরখে আকুল ভেল,
জর জর রিঝসে দুখ জ্বালা সব
দূর দূর চলি গেল।
মরমে বহই বসন্তসমীরণ,
মরমে ফুটই ফুল,
মরমকুঞ্জ'পর বোলই কুহু কুহু
অহরহ কোকিলকুল।
সখি রে উছসত প্রেমভরে অব
ঢলঢল বিহ্বল প্রাণ,
নিখিল জগত জনু হরখ-ভোর ভই
গায় রভসরসগান।
বসন্তভূষণভূষিত ত্রিভুবন
কহিছে—দুখিনী রাধা,
কঁহি রে সো প্রিয়, কঁহি সো প্রিয়তম,
হৃদিবসন্ত সো মাধা?
ভানু কহত অতি গহন রয়ন অব,
বসন্তসমীর শ্বাসে
মোদিত বিহ্বল চিত্তকুঞ্জতল
ফুল্ল বাসনা-বাসে।

1

Spring at last! The amuyās flare,
half-opened, trembling with bees.
A river of shadow flows through the grove.
I'm thrilled, dear trusted friend,
shocked by this pleasure-flame—
am I not a flame in his eyes?
His absence tears at me—
love blooms, and then spring
blows the petals from the world.
In my heart's grove the cuckoos pour out
a bewildering fountain of pleasure-drops,
jewels of the universe.
Even the bee-opened flowers mock me:
"Where's your lover, Rādhā?
Does he sleep without you
on this scented night of spring?"

I know he breathes secrets to you—
I can see their perfumes still dispersing
among the leaves of your longing.
Have I no memory of my own?
Besides, your head is full of flowers.
Go wait for him in the last shreds
of your innocence, crazy girl,
until grief comes for you.

২

শুনহ শুনহ বালিকা,
রাখ কুসুমমালিকা,
কুঞ্জ কুঞ্জ ফেরনু সখি শ্যামচন্দ্র নাহি রে।
দুলই কুসুমমুঞ্জরী,
ভমর ফিরই গুঞ্জরী
অলস যমুন বহয়ি যায় ললিত গীত গাহি রে।
শশিসনাথ যামিনী,
বিরহবিধুর কামিনী,
কুসুমহার ভইল ভার হৃদয় তার দাহিছে।
অধর উঠই কাঁপিয়া
সখিকরে কর আপিয়া,
কুঞ্জভবনে পাপিয়া কাহে গীত গাহিছে।
মৃদু সমীর সঞ্চলে
হরয়ি শিথিল অঞ্চলে,
চকিত হৃদয় চঞ্চলে কাননপথ চাহি রে।
কুঞ্জপানে হেরিয়া,
অশ্রুবারি ডারিয়া
ভানু গায় শূন্যকুঞ্জ শ্যামচন্দ্র নাহি রে!

2

You innocent,
so careless with your lapful of red flowers,
eyes searching the moonless woods
for his eyes looking back.
Not there tonight. No sound but the bees
rummaging through the twilight, whispering.
You startle like a deer, Rādhā.

Where will she quench herself,
this flower-burdened girl?
I have no unguent for her burning.
No hands but his can cure her,
no hands but his can catch
her chain of flowers and hold her still.

She grabs my hand, not knowing
it's mine, night bird about to cry out
to the whole forest, since she can't see him
or feel the after-tremor of his touch
subsiding in her body.

Look, the wind's undressing you,
scattered moonbeam, hold still—
it's not *his* longing that loosens the cloth.
Talk to me, tear-spangled one,

quit looking down the empty path.
It's late, it's dark. Not even his shadow lies there.
Be quiet now. I'll sing to you.

৩

হৃদয়ক সাধ মিশাওল হৃদয়ে,
কণ্ঠে বিমলিন মালা।
বিরহবিষে দহি বহি গল রয়নী,
নহি নহি আওল কালা।
বুঝনু বুঝনু সখি বিফল বিফল সব,
বিফল এ পীরিতি লেহা—
বিফল রে এ মঝু জীবন যৌবন,
বিফল রে এ মঝু দেহা!
চল সখি গৃহ চল, মুঞ্চ নয়ন-জল,
চল সখি চল গৃহকাজে,
মালতি-মালা রাখহ বালা,
ছি ছি সখি মরু মরু লাজে।
সখি লো দারুণ আধি-ভরাতুর
এ তরুণ যৌবন মোর,
সখি লো দারুণ প্রণয়-হলাহল
জীবন করল অঘোর।
তৃষিত প্রাণ মম দিবস-যামিনী
শ্যামক দরশন আশে,
আকুল জীবন থেহ ন মানে,
অহরহ জ্বলত হুতাশে।

সজনি, সত্য কহি তোয়,
খোয়ব কব হম শ্যামক প্রেম
সদা ডর লাগয়ে মোয়।

3

He never came to me.
In the whole long dark he never came
to tend my lacerated heart.
I'm a girl with nothing, a tree
with neither flowers nor fruit.

Go home, poor tragedy. Distract yourself
with chores, dry your eyes. Go on now,
dear tattered garland, limp with shame.

How can I bear this staggering weight?
I'm budding and blooming at once,
and dying, too, crushed by thirst
and the leaves' incessant rustling.
I need his eyes in mine, their altar's gold fire.
Don't lie to me. I'm lost in that blaze.
My heart waits, fierce and alone.
He'll leave me. If he leaves me, I'll poison myself.

He drinks at love's fountain, too,
my friend. His own thirst will call him.
Listen to Bhānu: a man's love
whets itself on absence if it's true.

হিয়ে হিয়ে অব রাখত মাধব,
সো দিন আসব সখি রে,
বাত ন বোলবে, বদন ন হেরবে,
মরিব হলাহল ভখি রে।
ঐস বৃথা ভয় না কর বালা,
ভানু নিবেদয় চরণে,
সুজনক পীরিতি নৌতুন নিতি নিতি,
নহি টুটে জীবন-মরণে।

৪

শ্যাম রে, নিপট কঠিন মন তোর।
বিরহ সাথি করি সজনী রাধা
রজনী করত হি ভোর।
একলি নিরল বিরল পর বৈঠত
নিরখত যমুনা পানে—
বরখত অশ্রু, বচন নহি নিকসত,
পরান থেহ ন মানে।
গহন তিমির নিশি ঝিল্লিমুখর দিশি
শূন্য কদম তরুমূলে,
ভূমিশয়ন 'পর আকুল কুন্তল,
কাঁদই আপন ভূলে।
মুগধ মৃগীসম চমকি উঠই কভু
পরিহরি সব গৃহকাজে
চাহি শূন্য 'পর কহে করুণ স্বর
বাজে রে বাঁশরি বাজে।
নিঠুর শ্যাম রে, কৈসন অব তুঁহুঁ
রহই দূর মথুরায়—
রয়ন নিদারুণ কৈসন যাপসি
কৈস দিবস তব যায়!
কৈস মিটাওসি প্রেম-পিপাসা
কঁহা বজাওসি বাঁশি?
পীতবাস তুঁহুঁ কথি রে ছোড়লি,
কথি সো বঙ্কিম হাসি?
কনক-হার অব পহিরলি কণ্ঠে,
কথি ফেকলি বনমালা?

4

That jewel-dark blue becomes you, Lord,
and rules your heart.
Rādhā sits alone and inconsolable as night
wrenches into dawn. Through veils of tears
she stares into the Yamunā's starry nothingness,
crazed by grief, by crickets.
She walks, she sits, she throws herself down
beneath the banyan, in the tryst-shadows,
a twig in her tangled hair. She cries
at a faraway flute, and leaves the floor unswept.

You're cruel, Lord of the lonely dark,
so far away in Mathurā.
In whose bed do you sleep?
Who slakes your thirst upon waking?
Where are your sun-colored clothes—
lost among the trees? And your crooked smile?
Whose necklace gleams on your neck?
Where have you thrown my wildflower chain?
My golden love for whom I bloom unseen,
you rule my emptiness, my endless nights.

For shame, black-hearted one—
you're coming with me.
That girl is suffering.

হৃদিকমলাসন শূন্য করলি রে,
কনকাসন কর আলা!
এ দুখ চিরদিন রহল চিত্তমে,
ভানু কহে, ছি ছি কালা!
ঝটিতি আও তুঁহুঁ হমারি সাথে,
বিরহ-ব্যাকুলা বালা।

৫

সজনি সজনি রাধিকা লো
দেখ অবহুঁ চাহিয়া,
মৃদুলগমন শ্যাম আওয়ে
মৃদুল গান গাহিয়া।
পিনহ ঝটিত কুসুম-হার,
পিনহ নীল আঙিয়া।
সুন্দরি সিন্দূর দেকে
সীঁথি করহ রাঙিয়া।
সহচরি সব নাচ নাচ
মিলন-গীত গাও রে,
চঞ্চল মঞ্জীর-রাব
কুঞ্জ গগন ছাও রে।
সজনি অব উজার মঁদির
কনক-দীপ জ্বালিয়া,
সুরভি করহ কুঞ্জভবন
গন্ধসলিল ঢালিয়া।
মল্লিকা চমেলি বেলি
কুসুম তুলহ বালিকা,
গাঁথ যূথি, গাঁথ জাতি,
গাঁথ বকুল-মালিকা।
তৃষিত-নয়ন ভানুসিংহ
কুঞ্জপথম চাহিয়া
মৃদুল গমন শ্যাম আওয়ে,
মৃদুল গান গাহিয়া।

5

Shake off that sadness, Rādhā!
Here comes your Lord, beautiful as sky,
sauntering and singing through the grove.
Quick, your indigo blouse.
Part your hair, reckless blossom,
deepen the red on your brow.

Let's celebrate the consummation!
With anklets jingling, run to the trysting-place,
light the golden oil,
perfume their secret room beneath the trees.
The star-white jasmine blooms tonight.
String a thousand flowers, girls,
and hang them all around.

Oh, my own thirst awakes
at the sight of him, the sound of him
practicing his song of their reunion.

৬

বঁধুয়, হিয়া 'পর আও রে,
মিঠি মিঠি হাসয়ি, মৃদু মধু ভাষয়ি,
হমার মুখ'পর চাও রে!
যুগ যুগ সম কত দিবস বহয়ি গল,
শ্যাম তু আওলি না,
চন্দ্র-উজর মধু-মধুর কুঞ্জ'পর
মুরলি বজাওলি না!
লয়ি গলি সাথ বয়ানক হাস রে,
লয়ি গলি নয়ন-আনন্দ!
শূন্য কুঞ্জবন, শূন্য হৃদয় মন,
কঁহি তব ও মুখচন্দ?
ইথি ছিল আকুল গোপ-নয়নজল,
কথি ছিল ও তব হাসি?
ইথি ছিল নীরব বংশীবটতট,
কথি ছিল ও তব বাঁশি;
তুঝ মুখ চাহয়ি শতযুগভর দুখ
নিমিখে ভেল অবসান।
লেশ হাসি তুঝ দূর করল রে
সকল মান-অভিমান।
ধন্য ধন্য রে ভানু গাহিছে
প্রেমক নাহিক ওর।
হরখে পুলকিত জগত-চরাচর
দুঁহুক প্রেমরস ভোর।

6

Come to me with a mouth full of words,
come look me in the face.
Śyāma—there I say aloud one of your tender names—
you laughing God, you did not come.
Your flute, that lonely bihaṅga,
stopped singing at the sight of moonlight
pouring honey on the grove.
What have you done with my innocence,
thief, where have you hidden my soul?
Did my river of tears not flow past your house?
Why did you not come to play your flute
here in the perfumed hallways of the trees?

O Lord, the lion of pride
slinks back into the shadows.
Your face undoes my pain.

How quickly she slips away, with nothing
but a thin sari of longing to protect her,
the two of them already laughing again.

Let's honor their sacred commingling.

৭

শুন সখি বাজত বাঁশি।
গভীর রজনী, উজল কুঞ্জপথ,
চন্দ্রম ডারত হাসি।
দক্ষিণ পবনে কম্পিত তরুগণ,
তম্ভিত যমুনা বারি,
কুসুম-সুবাস উদাস ভইল, সখি,
উদাস হৃদয় হমারি।
বিগলিত মরম, চরণ খলিত-গতি,
শরম ভরম গয়ি দূর,
নয়ন বারি-ভর, গরগর অন্তর,
হৃদয় পুলক-পরিপূর।
কহ সখি, কহ সখি, মিনতি রাখ সখি,
সো কি হমারই শ্যাম?
মধুর কাননে মধুর বাঁশরি
বজায় হমারি নাম?
কত কত যুগ সখি পুণ্য করনু হম,
দেবত করনু ধেয়ান,
তব ত মিলল সখি শ্যাম-রতন মম,
শ্যাম পরানক প্রাণ।
শ্যাম রে,
শুনত শুনত তব মোহন বাঁশি
জপত জপত তব নামে,
সাধ ভইল ময়্ দেহ ডুবায়ব
চাঁদ-উজল যমুনামে!

7

Listen, can you hear it?
His bamboo flute speaks
the pure language of love.
The moon enlightens the trees,
the path, the sinuous Yamunā.
Oblivious of the jasmine's scent
I stagger around,
disheveled heart bereft of modesty,
eyes wet with nerves and delight.
Tell me, dear friend, say it aloud:
is he not my own Dark Lord Śyāma?
Is it not my name his flute pours
into the empty evening?

For eons I longed for God,
I yearned to know him.
That's why he has come to me now,
deep emerald Lord of my breath.
O Śyāma, whenever your faraway flute thrills
through the dark, I say your name,
only your name, and will my body to dissolve
in the luminous Yamunā.

চলহ ত্বরিত গতি শ্যাম চকিত অতি,
ধরহ সখীজন হাত,
নীদ-মগন মহী, ভয় ডর কছু নহি,
ভানু চলে তব সাথ।

Go to her, Lord, go now.
What's stopping you?
The earth drowns in sleep.
Let's go. I'll walk with you.

৮

গহন কুসুম-কুঞ্জ মাঝে
মৃদুল মধুর বংশি বাজে,
বিসরি ত্রাস লোকলাজে
সজনি, আও আও লো।
অঙ্গে চারু নীল বাস,
হৃদয়ে প্রণয় কুসুম রাশ,
হরিণ-নেত্রে বিমল হাস,
কুঞ্জ বনমে আও লো॥
ঢালে কুসুম সুরভ-ভার,
ঢালে বিহগ সুরব-সার,
ঢালে ইন্দু অমৃত ধার
বিমল রজত ভাতি রে।
মন্দ মন্দ ভৃঙ্গ গুঞ্জে,
অযুত কুসুম কুঞ্জে কুঞ্জে,
ফুটল সজনি পুঞ্জে পুঞ্জে
বকুল যূথি জাতি রে॥
দেখ সজনি শ্যামরায়,
নয়নে প্রেম উথল যায়,
মধুর বদন অমৃত সদন
চন্দ্রমায় নিন্দিছে;
আও আও সজনি-বৃন্দ,
হেরব সখি শ্রীগোবিন্দ,
শ্যামকো পদারবিন্দ
ভানুসিংহ বন্দিছে॥

8

He's there among the scented trees,
playing the notes he has taught you.
Too late for embarrassment, shy doe
nibbling at the forest's edge,
shawled in deep blue shadows.
He's calling you. The flower of your soul
is opening, little deer.
The river of scent will lead you
deep into the trees where he waits.
The bihaṅga also plays tonight—
do you hear his more distant flute?
Black bees carry the moon's luster
from flower to flower.
The rest of the grove will bloom tonight, I think.
How he looks at you, young animal.
He shames the moon with his own dark light.

Let's bow down before the young Lord,
the deep blue flowers of his feet.

৯

সতিমির রজনী, সচকিত সজনী
শূন্য নিকুঞ্জ অরণ্য।
কলয়িত মলয়ে, সুবিজন নিলয়ে
বালা বিরহ বিষণ্ণ!
নীল অকাশে, তারক ভাসে
যমুনা গাওত গান,
পাদপ মরমর, নির্ঝর ঝরঝর
কুসুমিত বল্লিবিতান।
তৃষিত নয়ানে, বন-পথ পানে
নিরখে ব্যাকুল বালা,
দেখ ন পাওয়ে, আঁখ ফিরাওয়ে
গাঁথে বন-ফুল মালা।
সহসা রাধা চাহল সচকিত
দূরে খেপল মালা,
কহল সজনি শুন, বাঁশরি বাজে
কুঞ্জে আওল কালা।
চকিত গহন নিশি, দূর দূর দিশি
বাজত বাঁশি সুতানে।
কণ্ঠ মিলাওল ঢলঢল যমুনা
কল কল কল্লোল গানে।
ভনে ভানু অব শুন গো কানু
পিয়াসিত গোপিনী প্রাণ।
তোঁহার পীরিত বিমল অমৃত রস
হরষে করবে পান।

9

A warm breeze frets through the woods,
the yearning darkness of the girl's house,
keeping her company.
Over the restless Yamunā's silver voices,
and the rustling, chafing voices of the vines,
blue stars drift.
There's thirst in Rādhā's eyes
longing down the pathway, seeing nothing,
thirst in her fingers stringing flowers.
She tosses the garland aside, whispering:

Listen, friend, can you hear it?
Kālā's flute pierces the forest's under-dark,
and the Yamunā's.

You listen, Kānu, Divine Lord among beasts,
she thirsts for the pure nectar of your love.
Let her drink.

১০

বজাও রে মোহন বাঁশী!
সারা দিবসক বিরহ-দহন-দুখ,
মরমক তিয়াষ নাশি।
রিঝ-মন-ভেদন বাঁশরি-বাদন
কঁহা শিখলি রে কান?
হানে থিরথির, মরম-অবশকর
লহু লহু মধুময় বাণ।
ধসধস করতহ উরহ বিয়াকুলু
ঢুলু ঢুলু অবশ-নয়ান;
কত কত বরষক বাত সোঁয়ারয়
অধীর করয় পরান।
কত শত আশা পূরল না বঁধু
কত সুখ করল পয়ান।
পহু গো কত শত পিরীত-যাতন
হিয়ে বিঁধাওল বাণ।
হৃদয় উদাসয়, নয়ন উছাসয়
দারুণ মধুময় গান।
সাধ যায় বঁধু, যমুনা-বারিম
ডারিব দগধ-পরান।
সাধ যায় পহু, রাখি চরণ তব
হৃদয় মাঝ হৃদয়েশ,
হৃদয়-জুড়াওন বদন-চন্দ্র তব
হেরব জীবনশেষ।
সাধ যায় ইহ চন্দ্রম-কিরণে,
কুসুমিত কুঞ্জবিতানে,

10

Your flute plays the exact notes of my pain.
It toys with me.
Where did you learn such stealth,
such subtle wounding, Kān?
The arrows in my breast
burn even in rain and wind.
Wasted moments pulse around me,
wishes and desires, departing happiness—
Master, my soul scorches.
I think you can see its heat in my eyes,
its intensity and cruelty. So let me drown
in the cool and consoling Yamunā,
or slake my desire in your cool,
consoling, changing-moon face.
It's the face I'll see in death.
Here's my wish and pledge:
that that same moon will spill its white pollen
down through the roof of flowers
into the grove, where I'll consecrate my life
to it forever, and be its flute-breath,
the perfume that hangs upon the air,
making all the young girls melancholy.
That's my prayer.

বসন্তবায়ে প্রাণ মিশায়ব,
বাঁশিক সুমধুর গানে।
প্রাণ ভৈবে মঝু বেণু-গীতময়,
রাধাময় তব বেণু।
জয় জয় মাধব, জয় জয় রাধা,
চরণে প্রণমে ভানু।

Oh, the two of you, way out of earshot.
If you look back you'll see me, Bhānu,
warming herself at the weak embers of the past.

১১

আজু সখি মুহু মুহু
গাহে পিক কুহু কুহু,
কুঞ্জবনে দুঁহু দুঁহু
দোঁহার পানে চায়।
যুবন মদ-বিলসিত,
পুলকে হিয়া উলসিত,
অবশ তনু অলসিত
মূরছি জনু যায়।
আজু মধু চাঁদনী
প্রাণ উনমাদনী,
শিথিল সব বাঁধনী,
শিথিল ভই লাজ।
বচন মৃদু মরমর,
কাঁপে রিঝ থরথর,
শিহরে তনু জরজর,
কুসুম-বন মাঝ।
মলয় মৃদু কলয়িছে,
চরণ নহি চলয়িছে,
বচন মুহু খলয়িছে,
অঞ্চল লুটায়।
আধফুট শতদল,
বায়ুভরে টলমল,
আঁখি জনু ঢলঢল
চাহিতে নাহি চায়।

11

High in the blossoming canopy,
the cuckoo repeats himself.
Below him, the two of them
swim in each other's eyes.
May I dispense with modesty, friends?
Look at their beautiful bodies.
In daylight or darkness, moving together
or at rest, they seem washed by some
honey-colored light. It's their own light,
rippling and shuddering over them.
Look—she's seeing him now,
and not just herself-with-him,
even though he's undoing
the knot she protects with her hand.
She's a half-bloomed lotus
disheveled by wind; even her eyes
are disheveled. Petals spiral from the clouds
into her hair, fall singed at her feet.
Cooling Yamunā, quenching moon—
this is my pain, too.

অলকে ফুল কাঁপয়ি
কপোলে পড়ে ঝাঁপয়ি,
মধু অনলে তাপয়ি
খসয়ি পড়ু পায়।
ঝরই শিরে ফুলদল,
যমুনা বহে কলকল,
হাসে শশি ঢলঢল
ভানু মরি যায়।

১২

শ্যাম, মুখে তব মধুর অধরমে
হাস বিকাশত কায়,
কোন স্বপন অব দেখত মাধব,
কহবে কোন্ হমায়!
নীদ-মেঘপর স্বপন-বিজলি সম
রাধা বিলসত হাসি।
শ্যাম, শ্যাম মম, কৈসে শোধব
তুঁহুক প্রেমঋণ রাশি।
বিহঙ্গ, কাহ তু বোলন লাগলি?
শ্যাম ঘুমায় হমারা,
রহ রহ চন্দ্রম, ঢাল ঢাল তব
শীতল জোছন-ধারা।
তারক-মালিনী সুন্দর যামিনী
অবহু ন যাও রে ভাগি,
নিরদয় রবি, অব কাহ তু আওলি
জ্বাললি বিরহক আগি।
ভানু কহত অব—রবি অতি নিষ্ঠুর
নলিন-মিলন অভিলাষে
কত রনারীক মিলন টুটাওত
ডারত বিরহ-হুতাশে।

12

I know who visits your dream, Dark One.
Say her name. Her smile streaks
like lightning through clouds of sleep.
Śyāma, she has nothing with which to repay you.

Such impatience, bihaṅga!
Don't wake my sleeping Śyāma.
And you, moon, pour down your cold milk
on the sun's too early fire.

Sometimes time is cruel in miniature,
as when dawn crowds the last hours.

১৩

সজনি গো,
শাঙন গগনে ঘোর ঘনঘটা
নিশীথ যামিনী রে।
কুঞ্জপথে সখি, কৈসে যাওব
অবলা কামিনী রে।
উন্মদ পবনে যমুনা তর্জিত
ঘন ঘন গর্জিত মেহ।
দমকত বিদ্যুত পথতরু লুণ্ঠত,
থরহর কম্পত দেহ।
ঘন ঘন রিম্‌ ঝিম্‌ রিম্‌ ঝিম্‌ রিম্‌ ঝিম্‌,
বরখত নীরদপুঞ্জ।
ঘোর গহন ঘন তাল তমালে
নিবিড় তিমিরময় কুঞ্জ।
বোল ত সজনী এ দুরুযোগে
কুঞ্জে নিরদয় কান
দারুণ বাঁশী কাহ বজায়ত
সকরুণ রাধা নাম।

সজনি,
মোতিম হারে বেশ বনা দে
সীঁথি লগা দে ভালে।
উরহি বিলোলিত শিথিল চিকুর মম
বাঁধহ মালত মালে।
খোল দুয়ার ত্বরা করি সখি রে,
ছোড় সকল ভয়লাজে,

13

Not only is it dark, but clouds roar
like the Yamunā, invisible and drenching;
lightning pillages the trees.
How can I see which way to go?
Alone I stand shaking in the dark hall
of the tamāla, its fan-leaves my only roof.

Tell me, is Kān in this heartless place?
Is that why his flute goes on playing
the notes of my name? Friend, I'm going.
Help me fix this jasmine in my hair.
Open the gate—I'll free my soul from its cage.

Don't fly, little bihaṅga. My fear
builds like the thunder. Don't go.

হৃদয় বিহগসম ঝটপট করত হি
পঞ্জর-পিঞ্জর মাঝে।
গহন রয়নমে ন যাও বালা
নওল কিশোরক পাশ।
গরজে ঘন ঘন, বহু ডর খাওব
কহে ভানু তব দাস।

১৪

বাদর বরখন, নীরদ গরজন,
বিজুলী চমকন ঘোর,
উপেখই কৈছে, আও তু কুঞ্জে
নিতি নিতি মাধব মোর।
ঘন ঘন চপলা চমকয় যব পহু
বজর পাত যব হোয়,
তুঁহুক বাত তব সমরয়ি প্রিয়তম
ডর অতি লাগত মোয়।
অঙ্গ-বসন তব, ভীঁখত মাধব
ঘন ঘন বরখত মেহ,
ক্ষুদ্র বালি হম, হমকো লাগয়
কাহ উপেখবি দেহ?
বইস বইস পহু কুসুমশয়ন ’পর
পদযুগ দেহ পসারি
সিক্ত চরণ তব মোছব যতনে
কুন্তলভার উঘারি।
শ্রান্ত অঙ্গ তব হে ব্রজসুন্দর
রাখ বক্ষ ’পর মোর,
তনু তব ঘেরব পুলকিত পরশে
বাহু মৃণালক ডোর।
ভানু কহে বৃকভানুনন্দিনী
প্রেমসিন্ধু মম কালা
তোঁহার লাগয় প্রেমক লাগয়
সব কছু সহবে জ্বালা।

14

When we're together, nights like this delight me.
But when the clouds come down between us
and thrash around so rudely in the trees,
then I fear, Lord, imagining your breath-taking words
lost out there among the swords of lightning.
Come, you're drenched, Mādhava,
drenched again, in these incessant rains.
Through the war of weather you've come to me.
Take off your clothes. Let me dry you. I'll untie my hair.
Come lie with me among the stalks of lotus,
skin cold and thrilled.

He's the whole dark ocean of love.
And for the sake of love,
each being shall burn its own small flame.

১৫

মাধব, না কহ আদর বাণী,
না কর প্রেমক নাম।
জানয়ি মুঝকো অবলা সরলা
ছলনা না কর শ্যাম।
কপট, কাহ তুঁহু ঝুট বোলসি
পীরিত করসি, তু মোয়?
ভালে ভালে হম অলপে চিহ্নু
না পতিয়াব রে তোয়।
ছিদল তরী সম কপট প্রেম ’পর
ডারনু যব মনপ্রাণ,
ডুবনু ডুবনু রে ঘোর সায়রে
অব কুত নাহিক ত্রাণ।
মাধব, কঠোর বাত হমারা
মনে লাগল কি তোর?
মাধব, কাহ তু মলিন করলি মুখ,
ক্ষমহ গো কুবচন মোর!
নিদয় বাত অব কবহুঁ ন বোলব
তুঁহু মম প্রাণক প্রাণ।
অতিশয় নির্মম, ব্যথিনু হিয়া তব
ছোড়য়ি কুবচন-বাণ।
মিটল মান অব—ভানু হাসতহি
হেরই পীরিত-লীলা।
কভু অভিমানিনী আদরিণী কভু
পীরিতি-সাগর বালা!

15

Don't talk about love to me, Mādhava.
Don't play rough games with my heart.
Why do you talk of love? Your words spill
as from a boat full of holes, and my soul
spills with them, beyond saving.

I'm plainspoken — does that shock you?
Oh, your mouth has been eating sorrow!
Mādhava, I hear my own harsh voice
and am ashamed. Forgive me
the sharp arrows of my words, unfeeling one —
ah, I see where one grazed your heart...

She plays her part well,
one minute flushed and melting,
the next a petulant tease —
an ocean of love all by herself!

১৬

সখি লো, সখি লো, নিকরুণ মাধব
মথুরাপুর যব যায়,
করল বিষম পণ মানিনী রাধা,
রোয়বে না সো, না দিবে বাধা,
কঠিন-হিয়া সই, হাসয়ি হাসয়ি
শ্যামক করব বিদায়।
মৃদু মৃদু গমনে আওল মাধা,
বয়ন-পান তছু চাহল রাধা,
চাহয়ি রহল স চাহয়ি রহল,
দণ্ড দণ্ড সখি চাহয়ি রহল,
মন্দ মন্দ সখি নয়নে বহল
বিন্দু বিন্দু জল-ধার।
মৃদু মৃদু হাসে বৈঠল পাশে,
কহল শ্যাম কত মৃদু মধু ভাষে,
টুটয়ি গইল পণ, টুটইল মান,
গদগদ আকুল ব্যাকুল প্রাণ,
ফুকরয়ি উছসয়ি কাঁদিল রাধা,
গদগদ ভাষ নিকাশল আধা,
শ্যামক চরণে বাহু পসারি,
কহল—শ্যাম রে, শ্যাম হমারি,
রহ তুঁহু, রহ তুঁহু, বঁধু গো রহ তুঁহু,
অনুখন সাথ সাথ রে রহ পঁহু,
তুঁহু বিনে মাধব, বল্লভ, বান্ধব,
আছয় কোন্ হমার!

16

When pitiless Mādhava left for Mathurā City,
in a fit of anger Rādhā made a vow.
Unsmiling, she sent him on his way,
berating his casual heart.
Off he went, his mouth full of sweet talk,
but Rādhā did not turn to see him go.
Instead she saw the face of her own sadness
forming and breaking all night
in the river of tears. Then his soft voice
sat down beside her ragged one,
and Rādhā broke her vow,
her voice bruised by grief,
her arms longing toward him, crying:

Stay, Śyāma, my love Śyāma, stay.
Stay with me. I have no friend but you,
no love, Mādhava. No one but you.

She wrapped her arms around his feet,
her face dissolving,
while he sat murmuring
the words she longed to hear.

পড়ল ভূমি 'পর শ্যামচরণ ধরি,
রাখল মুখ তছু শ্যামচরণ 'পরি,
উছসি উছসি কত কাঁদয়ি কাঁদয়ি
রজনী করল প্রভাত।
মাধব বৈসল মৃদু মধু হাসল,
কত অশোয়াস বচন মিঠ ভাষল,
ধরইল বালিক হাত।
সখি লো, সখি লো বোল ত সখি লো
যত দুখ পাওল রাধা,
নিঠুর শ্যাম কিয়ে আপন মনমে
পাওল তছু কছু আধা?
হাসয়ি হাসয়ি নিকটে আসয়ি
বহুত স প্রবোধ দেল,
হাসয়ি হাসয়ি পলটয়ি চাহয়ি
দূর দূর চলি গেল।
অব সো মথুরাপুরক পন্থমে,
ইঁহ যব রোয়ত রাধা,
মরমে কি লাগল তিলভর বেদন
চরণে কি তিলভর বাধা?
বরখি আঁখিজল ভানু কহে — অতি
দুখের জীবন ভাই।
হাসিবার তর সঙ্গ মিলে বহু
কাঁদিবার কো নাই।

Rādhā, talk to me, dear friend.
Ask yourself: has Śyāma himself
ever felt such pain as this?

He came to her laughing, and now
he throws that same laugh back
over his shoulder as he leaves for Mathurā.
Not a grain of compassion clings to his feet.
Who knows how long he'll stay?

Weeping for Rādhā, I say that life is pain.
If there were no love, there would be no grief.

১৭

বার বার সখি বারণ করনু
　　　　ন যাও মথুরা ধাম।
বিসরি প্রেমদুখ, রাজভোগ যথি
　　　　করত হমারই শ্যাম।
ধিক তুঁহু দাম্ভিক, ধিক রসনা ধিক,
　　　　লইলি কাহারই নাম?
বোল ত সজনি, মথুরা অধিপতি
　　　　সো কি হমারই শ্যাম?
ধনকো শ্যাম সো, মথুরা পুরকো,
　　　　রাজ্য মানকো হোয়,
নহ পীরিতিকো, ব্রজ কামিনীকো,
　　　　নিচয় কহনু ময় তোয়।
যব তুঁহু ঠারবি, সো নব নরপতি
　　　　জনি রে করে অবমান,
ছিন্ন কুসুমসম ঝরব ধরা 'পর,
　　　　পলকে খোয়ব প্রাণ।
বিসরল বিসরল সো সব বিসরল
　　　　বৃন্দাবন সুখসঙ্গ,
নব নগরে সখি নবীন নাগর
　　　　উপজল নব নব রঙ্গ।
ভানু কহত — অয়ি বিরহকাতরা
　　　　মনমে বাঁধহ থেহ।
মুগুধা বালা, বুঝই বুঝলি না,
　　　　হমার শ্যামক লেহ।

17

So many times, Lord, I have implored you
to forsake the pleasures of Mathurā and
not leave me here to grieve alone.
So many times, Śyāma.

Rādhā, your tongue will get you
into trouble. Be careful whose name
you take for granted.

But isn't he my beautiful, rich, honored
Lord of the city towers, my own Dark King,
Śyāma?

Steady yourself, friend.
Do you think no girls like you
wait for him in the gardens of the town,
imagining how they will pleasure him?
You're not his one and only.
If you called him to you now,
your voice loud in the grove,
and he declined you,
you would split like a *kusuma* bud
thrown down at his feet.
He's the heat of the conversation
in the town; all the girls know his name.

Be calm and patient. Believe me,
you endanger yourself, for you know
nothing of the real Śyāma's love.

১৮

হম যব না রব সজনী,
নিভৃত বসন্ত-নিকুঞ্জ-বিতানে
আসবে নির্মল রজনী,
মিলন-পিপাসিত আসবে যব সখি
শ্যাম হমারি আশে,
ফুকারবে যব রাধা রাধা
মুরলী উরধ শ্বাসে,
যব সব গোপিনী আসবে ছুটই
যব হম আসব না;
যব সব গোপিনী জাগবে চমকই
যব হম জাগব না,
তব কি কুঞ্জপথ হমারি আশে
হেরবে আকুল শ্যাম?
বন বন ফেরই সো কি ফুকারবে
রাধা রাধা নাম?
না যমুনা, সো এক শ্যাম মম
শ্যামক শত শত নারী;
হম যব যাওব শত শত রাধা
চরণে রহবে তারি।
তব সখি যমুনে, যাই নিকুঞ্জে,
কাহ তয়াগব দে?
হমারি লাগি এ বৃন্দাবনমে
কহ সখি, রোয়ব কে?

18

How long must I go on waiting
under the secretive awnings of the trees?
When will he call the long notes of my name
with his flute: Rādhā, Rādhā, so full of desire
that all the little cowherd-girls will start awake
and come looking for him, as I look for him.
Will he not come to me,
playing the song of Rādhā with his eyes and hands?
He will not, Yamunā.
I have one moon—Śyāma—
but a hundred Rādhās yearn for moonlight at his feet.
I'll go to the grove, companion river.
Alone, I'll honor our trysting-place.
No one will make me renounce it.

Come with me into the dark trees.
You'll have your tryst,
its trembling raptures and its tears.

ভানু কহে চুপি — মানভরে রহ
আও বনে ব্রজ-নারী,
মিলবে শ্যামক থরথর আদর
ঝরঝর লোচন বারি।

১৯

মরণ রে,
তুঁহু মম শ্যাম সমান।
মেঘ বরণ তুঝ, মেঘ জটাজুট,
রক্ত কমল কর, রক্ত অধর-পুট,
তাপ-বিমোচন করুণ কোর তব,
মৃত্যু অমৃত করে দান।
তুঁহু মম শ্যাম সমান।
মরণ রে,
শ্যাম তোঁহারই নাম,
চির বিসরল যব নিরদয় মাধব
তুঁহু ন ভইবি মোয় বাম।
আকুল রাধা রিঝ অতি জরজর,
ঝরই নয়ন দউ অনুখন ঝরঝর,
তুঁহু মম মাধব, তুঁহু মম দোসর,
তুঁহু মম তাপ ঘুচাও,
মরণ তু আও রে আও।
ভুজ পাশে তব লহ সম্বোধয়ি,
আঁখিপাত মঝু আসব মোদয়ি,
কোর উপর তুঝ রোদয়ি রোদয়ি,
নীদ ভরব সব দেহ।
তুঁহু নহি বিসরবি, তুঁহু নহি ছোড়বি,
রাধা-হৃদয় তু কবহুঁ ন তোড়বি
হিয় হিয় রাখবি অনুদিন অনুখন
অতুলন তোঁহার লেহ।

19

You resemble my Dark Lord Śyāma,
Death, with your red mouth
and unkempt hair, dressed in cloud.
Sheltered in your lap, my pain abates.
You are the fountain of nectar, Death,
of immortality. I say aloud
the perfect word of your name.
Mādhava has forgotten Rādhā.
But you, Dark Lord, accomplice,
you will not abandon me.
Call me now. I'll come into your arms
in tears, but soon lapse into half-closed sleep,
drowsy with bliss, my pain erased.
You won't forget me.
I hear a flute from the distant playgrounds,
the city far away—it must be yours,
for it plays my name.

Now darkness comes on, and with it a storm.
Clouds roil, and lightning slashes at the palms;
the desolate path twists into darkness.
I'm fearless now. I'll meet you there, Death,
in the old trysting-place. I know the way.

দূর সঙে তুঁহু বাঁশি বজাওসি,
অনুখন ডাকসি, অনুখন ডাকসি
রাধা রাধা রাধা,
দিবস ফুরাওল, অবহুঁ ম যাওব,
বিরহ তাপ তব অবহুঁ ঘুচাওব,
কুঞ্জ-বাটপর অবহুঁ ম ধাওব
সব কছু টুটইব বাধা।
গগন সঘন অব, তিমির মগন ভব,
তড়িত চকিত অতি, ঘোর মেঘ রব,
শাল তাল তরু সভয় তবধ সব,
পন্থ বিজন অতি ঘোর—
একলি যাওব তুঝ অভিসারে,
যা'ক পিয়া তুঁহু কি ভয় তাহারে,
ভয় বাধা সব অভয় মূরতি ধরি,
পন্থ দেখাওব মোর।
ভানুসিংহ কহে—ছিয়ে ছিয়ে রাধা
চঞ্চল হৃদয় তোহারি
মাধব পহু মম, পিয় স মরণসেঁ
অব তুঁহু দেখ বিচারি।

Shame on your faithlessness, Rādhā.
Death is not another name for love.
You'll learn for yourself.

২০

কো তুঁহু বোলবি মোয়!
হৃদয়-মাহ মঝু জাগসি অনুখন,
আঁখ উপর তুঁহু রচলহি আসন,
অরুণ নয়ন তব মরম সঙে মম
নিমিখ ন অন্তর হোয়।
কো তুঁহু বোলবি মোয়!

হৃদয় কমল তব চরণে টলমল,
নয়ন যুগল মম উছলে ছলছল,
প্রেমপূর্ণ তনু পুলকে ঢলঢল
চাহে মিলাইতে তোয়।
কো তুঁহু বোলবি মোয়!

বাঁশরি ধ্বনি তুহ অমিয় গরল রে,
হৃদয় বিদারয়ি হৃদয় হরল রে,
আকুল কাকলি ভুবন ভরল রে,
উতল প্রাণ উতরোয়।
কো তুঁহু বোলবি মোয়!

হেরি হাসি তব মধুঋতু ধাওল,
শুনয়ি বাঁশি তব পিককুল গাওল,
বিকল ভ্রমরসম ত্রিভুবন আওল,
চরণ-কমল যুগ ছোঁয়।
কো তুঁহু বোলবি মোয়!

20

Who are You, who keeps my heart awake?
Every moment is lit by You, so that I feel
no longer separate from You.

Whose flute is playing sweet and bitter
songs of love? It starts the cuckoos singing,
and calls the nectar-heavy bees of my desire.

A young wife could be blooming
in the season of honey, watching the moon,
and be stolen in a moment.

Touch Rādhā, Whoever You are. She shivers
at Your feet, risking everything to bear
love's searing fire. Master, is that not You?

She's grown reckless with her soul.
Her fear is gone, her hesitation. Who are You?
She'll weep at Your lotus feet until she knows.

গোপবধূজন বিকশিত যৌবন,
পুলকিত যমুনা, মুকুলিত উপবন,
নীল নীর 'পর ধীর সমীরণ,
পলকে প্রাণমন খোয়।
কো তুঁহু বোলবি মোয়!

তৃষিত আঁখি, তব মুখ 'পর বিহরই,
মধুর পরশ তব, রাধা শিহরই,
প্রেম-রতন ভরি হৃদয় প্রাণ লই
পদতলে অপনা থোয়।
কো তুঁহু বোলবি মোয়!

কো তুঁহু কো তুঁহু সব জন পুছয়ি,
অনুদিন সঘন নয়নজল মুছয়ি,
যাচে ভানু, সব সংশয় ঘুচয়ি,
জনম চরণ 'পর গোয়।
কো তুঁহু বোলবি মোয়!

২১

সখিরে—পিরীত বুঝবে কে?
আঁধার হৃদয়ক দুঃখ কাহিনী
বোলব, শুনবে কে?
রাধিকার অতি অন্তর বেদন
কে বুঝবে অয়ি সজনী
কে বুঝবে সখি রোয়ত রাধা
কোন দুখে দিন রজনী?
কলঙ্ক রটায়ব জনি সখি রটাও
কলঙ্ক নাহিক মানি,
সকল তয়াগব লভিতে শ্যামক
একঠো আদর বাণী।
মিনতি করিলো সখি শত শত বার, তু
শ্যামক না দিহ গারি,
শীল মান কুল, অপনি সজনি হম
চরণে দেয়নু ডারি।
সখিলো—
বৃন্দাবনকো দুরুজন মানুখ
পিরীত নাহিক জানে,
বৃথাই নিন্দা কাহ রটায়ত
হমার শ্যামক নামে?
কলঙ্কিনী হম রাধা, সখিলো
ঘৃণা করহ জনি মনমে
ন আসিও তব্ কবহুঁ সজনিলো
হমার আঁধা ভবনমে।

21

Who wants to hear the long, miserable
story of Rādhā? Who among you
fathoms love's mystery?
The world will see my disgrace, my stain of love,
but I won't care. I'll abandon myself
for one caress from Śyāma.

I've asked you and asked you, my friends,
not to revile him, for I have risked
everything for him: my family's honor,
my friendships, my soul.
All these I pour out in sacrifice at his feet.

I know that men from the town slander
my Dark Lord's name. They know nothing of love.
If my blunt words offend you, then don't follow me
into my heart's dark trysting-place.

Now you understand my own heart,
which bore long ago the fire that sears you.
Flames still flare up, in both body and mind.

কহে ভানু অব—বুঝবে না সখি
কোহি মরমকো বাত,
বিরলে শ্যামক কহিও বেদন,
বক্ষে রাখয়ি মাথ!

২২

হম সখি দারিদ নারী!
জনম অবধি হম পীরিতি করনু
মোচনু লোচন-বারি।
রূপ নাহি মম, কছুই নাহি গুণ
দুখিনী আহির জাতি,
নাহি জানি কছু বিলাস-ভঙ্গিম
যৌবন গরবে মাতি।
অবলা রমণী, ক্ষুদ্র হৃদয় ভরি
পীরিত করনে জানি;
এক নিমিখ পল, নিরখি শ্যাম জনি
সোই বহুত করি মানি।
কুঞ্জ পথে যব নিরখি সজনি হম,
শ্যামক চরণক চীনা,
শত শত বেরি ধূলি চুম্বি সখি,
রতন পাই জনু দীনা।
নিঠুর বিধাতা, এ দুখ-জনমে
মাঙব কি তুয়া পাশ!
জনম অভাগী, উপেখিতা হম,
বহুত নাহি করি আশ—
দূর থাকি হম রূপ হেরইব,
দূরে শুনইব বাঁশি।
দূর দূর রহি সুখে নিরীখিব
শ্যামক মোহন হাসি।
শ্যাম-প্রেয়সি রাধা! সখিলো!
থাক' সুখে চিরদিন!

22

I've fallen from my life, friend—
my tears since birth have washed my charms away.
But I've known pure love.
If I glimpse for an instant
my own Dark Lord on the forest path,
I kiss the dust at his feet a hundred times,
as if each grain were a jewel.

Unlucky, star-crossed birth.
I long only to stay within the shadow
of his flute and taste from afar his dark smile.

Rādhā is the Dark Lord's Mistress!
May her pleasure be endless!

But it's grief that's endless,
a river of unseen tears.

Is your indifference endless also, Black One?
Its half-bloomed flowers fall unseen
into the river of human tears.

তুয়া সুখে হম রোয়ব না সখি
অভাগিনী গুণ হীন।
অপন দুখে সখি, হম রোয়ব লো,
নিভৃতে মুছইব বারি।
কোহি ন জানব, কোন বিষাদে
তন-মন দহে হমারি।
ভানু সিংহ ভনয়ে, শুন কালা
দুখিনী অবলা বালা—
উপেখার অতি তিখিনী বাণে
না দিহ না দিহ জ্বালা।

Postscript

1. Tagore and His Poetry [2]

Rabindranath Tagore (1861–1941) wrote in a colonial Bengal that was alternately torn between a desire to live up to the European standards of modernity, thrust upon it by the British, and the population's own sense of brooding nationalism that sought independence for an ancient culture revived. In this heady period Tagore's family was among the most prominent in Calcutta, his grandfather Dwarkanath (1794–1846) having created a financial empire in banking and trade with the British and, with the proceeds, purchased large *zamandari* estates in east Bengal and Orissa. Tagore's father, Debendranath (1817–1905), was nearly as shrewd a businessman as his father, maintaining the estates and solidifying the family fortune. But Debendranath was also a deeply religious man in a thoroughly modern way: he was a founding member of the Brahmo Samaj, a group of intellectuals who sought to distill India's complex religious heritage into a nonsectarian perspective that embraced Hindus, Muslims, Buddhists, and Christians, favoring

2. For this background, the reader is directed to several sources. A highly laudatory literary biography of Tagore is Krishna Kripalani's *Rabindranath Tagore: A Biography* (London: Oxford University Press, 1962). For a somewhat less worshipful presentation, see E. J. Thompson, *Rabindranath: Poet and Dramatist,* 2d revised edition (Oxford: Oxford University Press, 1948). For a more recent controversial political biography, see Krishna Dutta and Andrew Robinson, *Rabindranath Tagore: The Myriad-Minded Man* (New York: St. Martin's Press, 1995). For a brief overview of the life and works, see Prabhat Kumar Mukherji, *Life of Tagore,* trans. Sisir Kumar Ghosh (Delhi: Hind Paper Pocket Books, 1975). Mukherji's Bengali biography is the chronotopical standard: *Rabīndrajīvanī o Rabīndrasāhitya Praveśika,* 4 vols. (Calcutta: Viśvabhārati Granthālaya, 1353–1371 B.S. [1946–1964]). For an early look at Tagore's life as he first appeared on the European literary scene, see Ernest Rhys, *Rabindranath Tagore: A Biographical Study* (New York: The Macmillan Company, 1915).

none. The philosophical impulse behind this movement was thoroughly that of classical Hindu *vedānta,* yet its founders were strongly akin in spirit to the Unitarians with whom they associated. Because of his personal discipline, his active religious life, and his devotion to the literatures of Sanskrit, Debendranath was known by the honorary title of Maharshi, Great Seer. It was this man who insisted that young Rabindranath steep himself in the religious texts of the Upaniṣads, with their formless, ineffable divinity unifying all of creation. Though publicly a Brahmo by choice, Debendranth was domestically traditional; he never abandoned his commitment to his status as a Brahmin; his position on caste ultimately divided the Brahmo Samaj itself. This assumption of privilege was passed on to Rabindranath, who struggled through his life with the conflict inherent to his aristocratic acceptance of a socially stratified society coexisting with his belief in the oneness of all humanity. This never-resolved tension would eventually percolate through every literary genre he touched.

When a young man, Rabindranath was schooled at home in the family mansion called Jorasanko, at no. 6, Dwarkanath Tagore's Lane in Calcutta. Though he tried formal schooling on four occasions, none stuck, and he was left in the hands of private tutors who coached him through the rigors of a novel educational experiment that sought to bridge the intellectual worlds of a Europe imbued with the glamour of science, and a classical India with its soul-nurturing philosophies. As trite as this division may appear today, it seems to have struck a chord in Tagore, who would spend the rest of his life trying to reconcile the two into a synthesis of East and West. How could it have been otherwise for someone so sensitive and gifted; he and his family were implicated completely in the colonial project, yet deeply committed to the treasures of India's own achievements. In this, Tagore, perhaps more than any other figure of the period, epitomizes the extremes of conflicting values that we recognize today as marks of the colonial experience.

Built in to his regimen of disciplined work and writing was an intellectually unstructured space created by his older brothers, especially Dwijendranath, Satyendranath, and Jyotirindranath (there were six brothers and two sisters in all), who encouraged one another to compose and perform music, dramas, and poetry, to write short stories and novels, and to paint. Out of this riot of activity, two other members of this extended household, Gaganendranath and Abanindranath, Tagore's nephews, would found the Bengal School of Indian art, Abanindranath ultimately taking pride of place. The Tagore brothers were as politically active as they were eccentric. Life in this extended family, an experience that was simultaneously disciplined and freewheeling, where servants often functioned as master more than an absent father, stimulated Rabindranath with an eclectic education that included everything from the classical Sanskrit poetry of Kālidāsa to modern science. But the outlet for much of Rabindranath's intellectual, especially literary, impulse lay in sharing his achievements with a receptive audience, for which he seldom lacked in this uncommon household. There was one who was special: a sensitive, if not intellectually accomplished, young woman named Kadambari, wife of his elder brother Jyotirindranath.

In a traditional Bengali family of this period, wives were generally younger than their husbands, sometimes considerably; it was acceptable, even encouraged, for a young woman to seek a special support among her husband's younger brothers still living in the household. The relationship is termed "joking"; it is familiar and intimate, not formal. And it was with Kadambari that Rabindranath first felt the presence of a woman, a presence that he cherished long after her suicide in 1884 at age twenty-three or twenty-four. Over the decades that followed he would dedicate books to her, use her to model some of his heroines (such as the famous Charu), and, many surmise, on occasion write to her when he assumed his anonymous, universal voice. Kadambari's pet name for Rabindranath was a synonym for Rabi, Bhānu. One can well imagine her powerful impact on a fourteen-year-old boy, perhaps prompting these first forays into love poetry. But one can just as easily imagine the need of the young adolescent to explore this heady subject with impersonal remove, if not impunity. Bhānusiṃha — a whimsical translation of his first and last names — gave him that freedom. The love depicted was sensual and emotional, certainly not sexually explicit, fraught with anxiety and longing, an undefinable urge to be in the presence of the beloved, but unsure of how that might be effected. The strategy of anonymity, of both the subject and object, would become an enduring feature of the elemental poetry best known to his Western audiences as mystical.

Writing from the busy confines of Jorasanko continued until the young Rabindranath made his first trip abroad, to visit England from late 1878 to early 1880, an eye-opening and not altogether pleasant experience for this young aristocrat suddenly faced with prejudices against the color of his skin and his Indian customs — tempered nevertheless by a social life available to a select few. His first book, *Sandhyā Saṅgīt* (*Evening Song*), was published in 1880 and was received with no little acclaim, most notably from Bankim Chandra Chatterjee, the leading author of the day. Little more than three years later he was married to a ten-year-old girl, Mrinalini, continuing the conservative practices of his father, who arranged the marriage. In early February, right before his marriage, he published a book of poems titled *Chabi o Gān* (*Pictures and Songs*), dedicated to his beloved Kadambari; within two months she would be dead by her own hand, from poison, perhaps opium. The simultaneous upheavals of marriage and death shook Tagore, and served to complicate further his already complicated interior landscape. Restlessness set in. For the remainder of his life he was incapable of staying rooted in a single abode or engaged in a single activity.

Rabindranath participated off and on in the public life of Calcutta, both literary and political, while privately tending to the twinned domestic responsibilities of family and estates. The books poured forth, and in 1890 he went abroad again, this time for two short months to the United Kingdom, whence he abruptly returned, apparently homesick. He would not return to England for more than twenty years. But that time away in London seemed to have precipitated for him a new poetry, which first appeared in the publication of *Manasi* (*The Lady of the Mind*) shortly after his return in 1890. At last came the wider recognition for which he clearly had begun to hunger. There are two features of this poetry that would recur in ever-refined ways for the rest of his life: a distinctly Bengali sensibility, nationalist and yet regionally distinct, coupled with a personal emotional landscape that hinted of his later fascination with his living, indwelling God. Over the next several decades, one would come to reflect the other, Bengal universalized for everyman.

It was also in this same year of 1890 that his father sent him unprepared to manage the estates in eastern Bengal and Orissa, a fortuitous move that opened a new world of nature and peasantry to the city-dwelling aristocrat. Living on his grandfather's elegantly appointed houseboat, which he dubbed *Padmā,* the name of the river on which she was originally moored, he wandered up and down the rivers that crisscrossed the estates. On these long sojourns sometimes lasting weeks on end, he discovered the intensity of the seasons, the vastness of rice paddies, the rhythms of rural life, and the alternating threat and serenity provided by the sweeping rivers of eastern Bengal. That landscape would imprint itself on Tagore's emotional world.

The business of management and the reverie of the land proved to be a salutary combination during the next decade. Although Bengali prose had been developing dramatically during the middle decades of the nineteenth century, in the 1890s Rabindranath essentially invented a new prose style for his short stories and novels. He incorporated numerous Sanskritic terms and roots to coin a new Bengali lexicon, while constantly experimenting with syntax and grammar. But it was the rhythm and music of his prose that captured the imagination as much as the microscopic gaze into this rural backwater, which land composed the bulk of the family estates. His was prose meant to be heard as much as read. In a span of five years he produced forty-four short stories, many published initially in the journal *Sādhanā,* which he was editing; six volumes of short stories would emerge by the turn of the century.[3] In these tales, the country not only presented itself metaphorically as emotion, it came to represent a nostalgia, for ancient India stumbling its way to a modernity forced onto it by the colonial domination of the British empire. By contrast, the city often invoked the hustle and bustle of that empire, a distinctly different way of life. He dragged his readers back and forth between them almost as much as he did his own family with his constant movement between Calcutta and Shelidah, his *zamandari*.

Tagore's poetry of the same period seemed to reach a maturity that broke free of convention, perhaps not coincidentally at the same time that his love affair with the folk music of Bengal took a definitive shape. Although familiar with the folk idiom in Calcutta, Tagore frequently encountered local boatmen and itinerant bards, their vast repertoire of traditional ballads reflecting the distinct regions of the Bengali-speaking world; and he was also entertained by the Bāuls and other religious mendicants, who wandered the countryside singing their special brand of mystical experience. The newly formed Baṅgīya Sāhitya Pariṣad, or Bengali Literary Academy, in Calcutta, had begun in earnest to collect folk songs, ballads, local plays, while at the same time collecting and standardizing the editing of poetic, epic and semi-epic, and religious manuscripts from the sixteenth to nineteenth centuries. Tagore supported and inspired many to pay close attention to these little-studied genres that he was encountering firsthand. His own musical talents were spurred by this close contact with rural musical forms particularly, and it was during this period that his distinctive musical style would be shaped into what today is considered a quintessentially Bengali genre that bears his name, *Rabīndrasaṅgīt*. The music was simple, the lyrics perhaps more so,

3. William Radice's introduction to the short stories is highly informative of this critical decade, the 1890s, and his translations capture much of the rhythms of this new style of prose; see Rabindranath Tagore, *Selected Short Stories*, trans. with an introduction by William Radice, revised edition (London: Penguin Books, 1994).

but the performance was dominated by virtuosity of vocalized emotion, which standard was set by Tagore himself, whose voice was legendary. The corpus today contains hundreds of songs and can be heard on every public occasion and in nearly every household.

During the Shelidah residency his poetry manifested a lyric quality that paralleled the musical shift in his prose of this period. But this poetry spoke with a searching inner voice that resonated with the rustic Bāul, who followed *maner mānuṣ,* "the man within the heart."[4] Outward ritual was rejected in favor of personal cultivation of direct connection with the divine, divinity that is found in nature and, perhaps most profoundly, in the emotional drama of human love. It is an old theme in Bengal, one that had earlier compelled the Vaiṣṇava poets who had been inspired by the sixteenth-century Bengali god-man Kṛṣṇa Caitanya. For Tagore, who began his literary career as an erstwhile Vaiṣṇava poet named Bhānu, allegorizing the soul's search for God in the love play of Rādhā and Kṛṣṇa, the mature version of this human-divine connection would inform his remaining poetry, much of it a meditation on his *jīvan devatā,* the "the living God within," his muse.

Leading up to his fateful trip to the United Kingdom and the United States in 1912 and '13, Tagore's stature finally began to catch up to his astonishing literary output. His plays, which were musicals or lyric dramas that included many songs, often spurred his poetry, perhaps not consciously, by giving him the opportunity to test their aural mettle. While furiously editing three different literary journals, he expanded the song repertoire that began life in his plays into volumes of poetry that would soon make him famous outside of India—most notable among them, *Gītāñjali* (*Song Offerings*). The English version of *Gitanjali* (written without diacritics) was translated and edited by Tagore himself,

4. For a look at the impact of the Bāuls on Tagore's personal theology and poetry, see Edward C. Dimock Jr., "Rabindranath Tagore: 'The Greatest of the Bāuls of Bengal,'" *Journal of Asian Studies,* vol. 19, no. 1 (Nov. 1959), reprinted in Edward C. Dimock Jr., *The Sound of Silent Guns and Other Essays* (New Delhi: Oxford University Press, 1989).

and arranged with minor emendations by W. B. Yeats.[5] Yeats nominated him for the Nobel Prize in Literature, which he won in 1913. Tagore's idealism seemed to appeal to the selection committee, but it was his mystical strain that produced such a strong response in Yeats and the reading public in Europe, the United States, and South America.

What was circulated as *Gitanjali* in the West was a selection from three different volumes of poetry from the years leading up to his trip: *Naivedya*, or *Leavings* (referring to the food offerings returned to devotees after being presented to the Lord), *Kheyā*, or *Ferry* (the ferry a common Bengali trope for navigating the rivers of life), and *Gītāñjali*, or *Song Offerings* (*añjali*, offering, is usually flower petals in cupped hands to the deity; the offering here being *gīta*, or song). Ironically, the selection of 103 prose poems is only a fraction of what was in the original *Gītāñjali* itself, because Tagore did not feel that English speakers would be capable of understanding the imagery native to Bengal. He edited heavily, not only in his selection, but in his translation, in effect creating an entirely new poetry in English that emphasized his spiritual, mystical side, the universal dimension of his very Bengali world. Rabindranath's decision to turn the familiar landscape of Bengal into something foreign—for instance the flat fields of paddy became rolling meadows—left Bengali readers wanting for what they had come to recognize as a Tagore trademark, and it skewed dramatically the impression of his poetry among English readers; Western audiences never saw the unique coupling of the Bengali landscape to his emotional world. It was a choice that would haunt him. Because of this overly mystical emphasis, he gained celebrity as a guru as well as a poet, feeding the banal dichotomy of material West and spiritual East, while inadvertently playing to European fascination with the ancient *rishi*, the seer.[6]

5. Rabindranath Tagore, *Gitanjali*, with an introduction by W. B. Yeats (London & New York: The Macmillan Company, 1913).
6. His own statements about religion can be found in two books of essays, delivered to Harvard in 1913 and Cambridge in 1930; the former a somewhat

Soon after that publication came two more volumes in Bengali in the same vein as *Gītāñjali,* but which should not be seen as simple extensions of the first: *Gītimālya* (*Garland of Songs*) and *Gītālī* (*Lyrics*). As was becoming evident in *Gītāñjali,* the songs of the boatmen of eastern Bengal and the wandering Bāuls shaped the music and the idiom of these poems. In these several volumes the reader became intimately familiar with Rabindranath's *antaryāmī,* or "indweller," as he accompanied this guide through the brooding skies and swelling waters of the monsoon floods. Following the lead of the Bāuls, the language of these poems is rife with the terms adopted by esoteric country mystics, an individualistic communion with a divinity immanent in the world and within every human being. All of these paths express a desire for liberation, described as "dead while alive" (*jyānte morā*); Rabindranath, too, articulated a wistful desire for such a state. To express this liberating sense he addressed Death personified. One is left to wonder about the increasing frequency of such references, for in the previous decade he had endured the death of his father Debendranath, his wife Mrinalini, his daughter Renuka, and his son Samindranath. These deaths weighed heavily. Considering Rabindranath's already well-developed fascination with mortality, the desire for a liberation of life from its worldly constraints, though never morbid, comes through clearly in the English version of *Gitanjali.*

From this point forward Tagore's poetic voice was, especially for his English readers, more or less fixed, and many feel the next period is rather poetically uninventive. He became much more of a public figure and in 1915 received a knighthood, which he would try unsuccessfully to renounce in political protest some four years later. This public life, which placed him on a world stage with

6. (cont.) rambling, poetic view of the formless absolute found in the Upaniṣads, as he saw it applied to his world; the latter a more cogent vision of the relationship of religion and aesthetics. See Rabindranath Tagore, *Sādhanā: The Realisation of Life* (New York: The Macmillan Company, 1913), and idem, *The Religion of Man,* The Hibbert Lectures for 1930 (London: George Allen & Unwin, 1931).

Gandhi and other leaders of the nationalist movement, gave him the profile sufficient to generate funds to create a university at one of his family estates in Santiniketan (Abode of Peace), near Bolpur outside of Calcutta. Although not as experimental and fragile as it was during Tagore's lifetime, today this university ranks as one of the finest private institutions in the subcontinent. As he toured the world to raise money for his world university, Visva Bharati, and its companion technical school at Sriniketan (Abode of Abundance), which was dedicated to agrarian reform, peripatetic cannot even begin to describe his restless movement. In the next twenty-five years he would visit more than thirty different countries; many of them, especially the United States and Britain, he would visit repeatedly. After a long lull of moderate poetic activity —though he did manage a number of major novels and novellas, numerous essays, and published letters—his trip to Argentina in 1924, where he stayed in the home of Victoria Ocampo, seemed to have reawakened the muse. He would persist in all genres for the remainder of his life, writing poetry up to the end. The very last of his poems he dictated on his deathbed. Unadorned and direct, they were posthumously published as his *Śeṣa Lekhā* (*Final Compositions*). Somehow, in the urgent movement from continent to continent, Rabindranath managed to return time and again to those little poems that began his publishing career, for they held a fascination for him like nothing else in his oeuvre. He would revise the Rādhā–Kṛṣṇa episodes of Bhānusiṃha for the last time within a few months of his death in 1941.

2. *About Kṛṣṇa, Rādhā, and the Gopīs: Bengali Vaiṣṇava Poetry*

The songs of Bhānu speak of the love of Kṛṣṇa, the Dark Lord, the cowherd lover of the young and guileless women of Braj. It is an old mythology, whose most prominent source is the tenth book of the Sanskrit *Bhāgavata Purāṇa*, which might have been compiled as early as the eighth or ninth centuries, but probably later; old Sanskrit texts are notoriously difficult to date because they are understood to be anonymous revelations of Truth rather than books with historical authors. The proper subject matter for this and other *Purāṇas* is the play of the gods. It is an activity whose point is often hidden from humans, who can only behold it as marvelous and awesome, in the old senses of those words. This activity is styled *līlā,* or play, a word that evokes the licking of flames, endlessly moving and brilliant, though unpredictable. The god most closely associated with this idea is Kṛṣṇa, the Dark One. He is Śyāma, that blackish emerald-blue-green color whose beauty and grace stagger anyone lucky enough to behold it. Those lucky ones today are his worshipers called Vaiṣṇavas, after one of his most ancient forms as Viṣṇu.

As far back as the *Bhagavad Gītā,* Hindu tradition has it that Kṛṣṇa descends to earth whenever the world languishes under the burden of sinful action, when humans lose sight of dharma, that is, of what is proper and good. The descent is called *avatāra,* an ancient Sanskrit word that is often wrongly construed as "incarnation," when it simply means to cross down from heaven to earth, to appear or be manifest. The flesh is not involved, so there is no carnal tinge. But in one of the great ironies of this tradition, Kṛṣṇa's actions as an adolescent are all about love — not some abstract or Platonic form, but the fleshy, lustful sort.

When he came to earth, Kṛṣṇa grew up in the region of Braj, in a village called Vṛndāvana, not far from the modern Indian city of Agra. He was raised by foster parents, Nanda and Yaśodā, who were affectionately indulgent. His early life was a giant frolic between cowherding duties and domestic chores; he and his brother played endless games with his cowherd friends and teased mercilessly the cowherd girls, called *gopīs*. His affairs with these girls speak to the pulsing heat of adolescence, bodies coming together in secret trysts, liaisons that risk for these young women a lifetime of opprobrium for the irresistible thrill of the moment.

The rainy season is the time for lovers, when the brooding landscape is suddenly fecund, reinvigorated from its desiccation brought on by the relentless heat of summer. It is especially during this season, when regular activity comes to a halt, that Kṛṣṇa calls the cowherd girls into the forest with the enchanting sound of his flute. The milkmaids can no more resist the temptation of Kṛṣṇa's beckoning flute than they can follow him, when he leaves Braj, to the man's world of the ancient capital city of Mathurā, there to embark on the next phase of his martial work as *avatāra,* the slaying of the demon king Kaṃsa. The *gopīs* are driven to distraction, willing to forfeit their honor, their names, their standing in the world for but a glimpse of this young paramour. In trysts on the banks of the river, in the *tamāla* groves, in stands of jungly wildflowers, he satisfies them all, inasmuch as it is possible to satisfy the insatiable. The young women feign resistance, but they always secretly thrill when Kṛṣṇa steals their clothes and makes them stand before him to beg, or when he multiplies himself so that each *gopī* imagines she alone is dancing with Kṛṣṇa in the famous round dance under the full moon. Though he loves them all, there is one he favors: the golden-complexioned Rādhā.

Rādhā has many rivals among these young women and is the envy of all: her love for Kṛṣṇa is so complete that he is as irresistibly attracted to her as she to him. She, in her selflessness, affords Kṛṣṇa the greatest pleasure, and so becomes the model for all lovers and all devotees of this fickle god. Rādhā's love is most deeply satisfying because it is complete, unpredictable to the point of being distractedly contrary or "crooked," ever-fresh. It is by the standards of this tradition perfect. She alone is truly worthy. Yet inherent in Rādhā's distracted and all-consuming love lies the inevitable immolation of emotion that results from burning too hot, too fast.

This heartache takes the form of a burning desire to possess the beloved, a longing that is like no other, yet colored with the knowledge that the object of desire can be only fleetingly embraced. Each of these girls, and Rādhā most of all, suffers through this torment when she cannot be with her lord; it is the elixir of love mixed with a dose of agony, much as the Greeks envisioned eros

7. For a wonderfully provocative, poetic reverie on the nature of eros as *glukupikron,* see Anne Carson, *Eros the Bittersweet: An Essay* (Princeton: Princeton University Press, 1986).

as *glukupikron,* the "sweet-bitter."[7] It is their common plight and binds them uniquely; it becomes their permanent ontological condition. The Vaiṣṇava poets who relive this ancient activity as part of their devotional calling pronounce this agony *viraha,* the pain of separation, the true condition of any lover, of any devotee. And through the heat of this agony, known vicariously through song and meditation, the devotee experiences a salvific transformation, using the intense quality of the aesthetic experience as a vehicle to encounter God. The ancient aestheticians described explicitly, though not graphically, the occasional and fleeting love-in-union, but they favored as the dominant trope its opposite, love-in-separation. The agonizing want, the *viraha,* that ensues from this separation, becomes the prevailing mood. Eventually Kṛṣṇa will leave these young women for the capital city of Mathurā and set about the business of his *avatāra,* slaying evil kings and demons, leading the forces of good to victory on the battlefield of the great civil war that was rendered in the epic *Mahābhārata.*

For centuries Vaiṣṇavas all over India have tended to focus on one or another aspect of their lord's life: his childhood exploits, his preadolescent play with his brother and other companions, or his warring days as Arjuna's charioteer in the great civil war. But Kṛṣṇa's Bengali devotees have always favored the erotic mode of his adolescence in the sleepy little town of Vṛndāvana on the banks of the Yamunā River. And it is this poetry of trysting unions and impatient longing that the adolescent Rabindranath first wrote. Many see the Vaiṣṇava sensibility as the foundation of Rabindranath's emotional landscapes, and the imagery certainly bears this out. Just how this aesthetic works is worth examining.

Bengali Vaiṣṇava poems are based on a concept called *rasa. Rasa* means variously "juice" or "sap," the life-giving force of something, which extends to include the notion of "essence," especially in relation to emotions. The point is not to experience the emotion directly, but to "savor" it, to "taste" its *rasa,* its essential core stripped of any contingencies that might diminish its force. It is a vicarious emotional practice, best experienced through idealized dramatic presentation in poetry, drama, and song, and, for the adept, in meditation. The skilled poet will manipulate the stories the audience knows so well, and in that process call forth a variety of emotions with which the devotee will learn to identify until they become part of his or her own nature. In a purely literary context, the manipulation will produce sensations of pleasure and pain, or joy and sorrow, but in this religious context the aesthetic experience — always one of love — becomes itself the vehicle for transcendence. The most powerfully transcendent experience, according to Bengali Vaiṣṇavas, is the love of Kṛṣṇa. It is this love that becomes the traditional focal point of poetic exploration, the poetry a living witness to that love.

Love of course is anything but monolithic. The great Vaiṣṇava theologian Rūpa Gosvāmī, writing in Sanskrit in the sixteenth century, discriminates five fundamentally different types of love, each of which is worthy as an approach to Kṛṣṇa, but which are not equal in satisfying him.[8] The different types might be understood by looking at particular roles people play in relation to the object of their love. A subject of a king will, for instance, love the king with awe and respect, while a servant might love that same king with a more intimate, personal devotion. Yet both remain vertically distant. Friends, too, have special privileges that only companionship affords: joking relations, physical contact, a special brand of honesty and sharing. There is a different and greater kind of intimacy that occurs between the king and his son. It is a love that allows the child to transgress boundaries impossible for others, for the child will be indulged to crawl in his lap, to pull his beard, to revel in his touch. But it is lovers who experience the

8. Rūpa Gosvāmī, *Bhaktirasāmṛtasindhu,* ed. with Bengali translation by Haridāsa Dāsa, with the commentaries *Durgasaṃgamanī-ṭīkā* of Jīva Gosvāmī, *Artharatnālpadīpikā* of Mukundadāsa Gosvāmī, and *Bhaktisārapradarśiṇī-ṭīkā* of Viśvanātha Cakravartī, 3d edition (Mathurā: Haribola Kuṭīra from Śri Kṛṣṇajanmasthāna, 495 G.A. [1981]), pp. 359–392. For a detailed summary and analysis of the devotionalism proposed by Rūpa, see S. K. De, *History of the Vaiṣṇava Faith and Movement in Bengal* (Calcutta: Firma KLM, 1961), pp. 166–224.

most complete forms of love. The erotic is considered the most complete because, in its full form, it subsumes the other types, standing atop the hierarchy of love not as different but encompassing, and it is driven ultimately by an unparalleled passion.[9] By being complete, it is the most satisfying to Kṛṣṇa.

In the late fifteenth century, Kṛṣṇa is understood to have appeared once again, this time in Bengal, in Nadiyā, just adjacent to the location of the Tagore family estates some several centuries later. His form was that of a Bengali Brahmin who took the religious name of Kṛṣṇa Caitanya (1486–1533), and it is this man who inspired the devotees to celebrate in song this extraordinary love of Rādhā and Kṛṣṇa. Caitanya was, so they believed, an androgyne, Rādhā and Kṛṣṇa fused into a single body. Emotionally and in coloration he was Rādhā, in physical form he was Kṛṣṇa: both lovers forever in union, forever in separation. The permutations of these conditions provide the emotional highs and lows of every love affair, and Caitanya taught that they constitute the very stuff of devotion. To experience the varied emotions of love is to be transformed, to be transported into the presence of the divine, as his devotees were by loving him. But human love pales when compared to a god's love, so the best most devotees can hope to do is to try to approximate what they cannot provide directly. For Vaiṣṇava devotees that approximation does not mean that they should envision themselves as *gopīs*; the *gopīs* provide an object of empathy. Through poetry and song, through meditation, the devotee befriends the *gopīs*, especially hoping to serve Rādhā, love's perfect embodiment. In the early stages of this devotion, the work is in the imagination; later this love is cultivated through disciplined meditation that transports the devotee into the mythical land of Braj. To aid and abet Rādhā's affairs with Kṛṣṇa the devotee must follow Caitanya's lead and become a woman in this emotional world. Because the devotee cannot presume "herself" worthy of Kṛṣṇa's amorous advances, a secondary and instru-

9. The Sanskrit terms are *śānta* (awe and respect), *dāsya* (servitude), *sakhya* (companionship), *vātsalya* (parental love), and *śṛṅgāra* (erotic love).

mental persona must be adopted. The devotee enters the cosmic drama either as a teenage, even preadolescent, girl who acts as handmaiden, or as a duenna who advises and consoles. Bhānu of Rabindranath's poetry is the latter.

3. About the Poems

After writing the initial batch of Bhānu songs, Rabindranath very neatly copied them and presented them to the editor, a friend of the family, of the literary journal *Bhāratī*. When asked about their provenance, Rabindranath led the editor to believe that he had found an old manuscript in the Brahmo Samaj's library, and after studying the songs realized that they were by an author he was fairly certain no literary historian had yet discovered. It was during this period that literary historians had begun the task of compiling, editing, and publishing many of the ancient texts of Bengal, which had even then a documentable literary history of more than six hundred years—some would say considerably longer—certainly the most prolific among the vernaculars of the subcontinent. The editor, so the story goes, was nonplussed that an author who had produced so many poems was unknown to him, yet excited at the prospect of the new discovery. The first batch was published in the journal in 1875, and by 1883 a total of thirteen poems had seen print there (songs 8–11, 13–19, 21, 22). The first edition of the *Bhānusiṃha Ṭhākurer Padāvalī* would appear a year later in 1884, and to that original set Rabindranath would add another eight songs (songs 1–7, 12). The last to be added would not appear until 1886 (song 20). Later, when his works were collected as *Rabīndra Racanāvalī* in 1939, some two years before his death, only twenty were included; Tagore chose to eliminate songs 21 and 22.[10] But the full set now circulates in the single-volume edition that bears the original name of their collection.[11]

10. Rabīndranāth Ṭhākura, *Rabīndra Racanāvalī*, 36 vols. (Calcutta: Viśvabhāratī Granthālaya, 1346 B.S. [1939]), vol. 2, pp. 1–27.

11. The poems have been published with notes regarding changes in a different edition, in Rabīndranāth Ṭhākurā, *Bhānusiṃha Ṭhākurer Padāvalī* (Calcutta: Viśvabhāratī Granthabibhāg, 1376 B.S. [1969]). The publication history can be found there, on pp. 107–108.

For a number of years he refused to acknowledge their authorship. No doubt family members (and, probably long before the ruse ended, the editor of *Bhāratī* as well) must have enjoyed the joke. When the first edition of the collected Bhānusiṃha was released, the fictional biography of the author simultaneously appeared in the journal *Navajīvana,* hinting in the text who the real author might be. It was a scathing indictment of the academic community that dripped with a special sarcasm regarding the practice of positivist history that was all the rage. (The full text of this fictional biography can be found in the Appendix). That he chose to reveal his authorship in this roundabout way not only reveals a wonderfully wicked sense of humor (something, incidentally, completely lost to English readers of Tagore), but suggests that another impulse may have driven him. From the very beginnings of this literary adventure, Rabindranath seems to have toyed with his readership, tantalizing them with the songs, drawing readers' attention and then just as quickly pushing the songs offstage. The deflections were too numerous: the twenty-first-century reader must consider that these songs held a special meaning for Rabindranath.

In choosing this medium, Rabindranath followed the lead of the most prominent poets of early and mid-nineteenth-century Bengal. Bankim Chandra Chatterjee and Michael Madhusudan Dutt had composed poetry about Kṛṣṇa and his love affairs, perhaps as a kind of *rite de passage* for young poets. While those poets tended to write in a version of old Bengali, Rabindranath, ever the polyglot, chose its ancient and artificial literary relative called Brajabuli, the language that was favored by the religious poets themselves. Those other nineteenth-century poets wrote in their own names, while the young Rabindranath wrote under a pseudonym, but for years denied it. When the press finally discovered that he was responsible for these songs, they quickly compared him to Thomas Chatterton (1752–1770), another child prodigy, whose "The Ryse of Peyncteynge yn Englande, wroten bie T. Rowleie. 1469 for Mastre Canynge" (March 1769) caused just such a controversy as a prank pulled on the scholarly community.[12] It would, of course, prove to be a face-saving strategy, shifting the focus to his precociousness and away from their own gullibility. Rabindranath seems to have liked that, for it allowed him to acknowledge the songs but to invite their dismissal as juvenilia. Rabindranath himself even bragged at one point that a young Bengali, Niśikānta Caṭṭopādhyāya, wrote a thesis that included an analysis of Bhānusiṃha's work. But that unproved allegation came much later, perhaps as a way of demonstrating that it was the Western style of scholarship that was suspect, one of Rabindranath's continuing complaints (a dissatisfaction that led to the creation of his experimental university at Santiniketan).[13] Again the reader was distracted, persuaded that the real value of these poems lay in their continued novelty, not in their personal perspective.

The perspective is, of course, decidedly complex, because the poems must be read in the light of other Vaiṣṇava poems dedicated to Rādhā and Kṛṣṇa; but because they are not done by a Vaiṣṇava devotee, they cannot be read apart from their author. The Vaiṣṇava form, however, has always clouded their reading, essentially blotting out the consideration of their perpetrator. The full extent of this hermeneutical complexity comes through when we examine the circumstances of their production and circulation. In brief, the poems were written by a fourteen-year-old Bengali male, writing in the late nineteenth century, who revised the text repeatedly until he was nearly eighty years old—well into the twentieth. By adopting the Brajabuli Vaiṣṇava form, he pretended to be a devotee of the sixteenth or seventeenth century who would have, through devotion and meditation, transformed himself into a woman. The poetry focused on the emotional distress of Rādhā in

12. Prabhat Mukherji, *Rābīndrajīvanī o Rabīndrasāhitya Praveśika*, vol. 1, pp. 68–71.

13. The previously cited author Prabhat Mukherji told me in an interview at Santiniketan, on 8 August 1976, that this alleged thesis was ostensibly submitted to a German university, but an exhaustive search of all theses submitted to all major universities in Germany at that time produced no corroboration.

her love for Kṛṣṇa, and the poet entered this miniature drama through the persona of her confidante and duenna, Bhānu. Unlike other Vaiṣṇava poets who used the names given them at initiation (that is, their "real" identities as devotees), Bhānu was a pseudonym in the Western sense; it did not at all reflect a religious commitment. The drama of the poetry into which Bhānu entered, however, took place in a mythical *Urzeit* before time itself, the cosmic play of Kṛṣṇa and Rādhā and the denizens of Braj. But unlike the more common form of authorial participation that tended to favor the image of a young eligible woman or even a preadolescent handmaiden of Rādhā and her friends, the fourteen-year-old Rabindranath entered the poems as a middle-aged woman, a woman who herself loved Kṛṣṇa but could only look on and commiserate. In this role, Bhānu proffers sage advice, the voice of a lifetime of experience.

A formal move sets these poems apart from their Vaiṣṇava models: Bhānu converses much more directly and frequently with Rādhā than is typical of the genre. The bulk of the content requires little explanation, for the situation emphasizes the univeral trauma of first love. How far should one go in reading them as Vaiṣṇava poems because of the form? A Vaiṣṇava would certainly read these poems as completely autobiographical, a revelation of the author's personal experience; this Rabindranath disavowed, but perhaps disingenuously, distancing himself from any explicit autobiographical connection by dismissing their religious "authenticity." In his English memoirs, titled *My Reminiscences,* he wrote:

> Whoever Bhanu Singha might have been, had his writings fallen into the hands of latter-day me, I swear I would not have been deceived. The language might have passed muster; for that which the old poets wrote in was not their mother tongue, but an artificial language varying in the hands of different poets. But there was nothing artificial about their sentiments. Any attempt to test Bhanu Singha's

> poetry by its ring would have shown up the base metal. It had none of the ravishing melody of our ancient pipes, but only the tinkle of a modern, foreign barrel organ.[14]

Underlying this alleged exercise in humility is an assumption that Rabindranath seems to have counted on to sway his readers: to be "authentic" the poetry had to have been written by a Vaiṣṇava, because the generation of poetic emotion is itself ontologically structured by the religious experience of the author. Rabindranath of course was no Vaiṣṇava, though Vaiṣṇava sensibilities regarding love certainly colored his emotional landscapes.

While the poems in all of their twenty-seven published renditions kept to the common core of *viraha,* the bittersweet longing of separation from the beloved, the poems did change over the course of Tagore's life. Originally they were specifically Vaiṣṇava in mood, with a strong emphasis on the erotic forms of love, though a love whose consummation the reader was left to imagine. Tracking the changes documented so lovingly by the editors of Visva Bharati Press in the last printed edition, one can chart a change taking place by degrees. There is a subtle increase in ambiguity, or, rather, less Vaiṣṇava specificity, a tendency to generalize and abstract from what was in earlier versions more precisely delineated. The dominant erotic mood subtly gives way to a humility in the face of unrequited love, especially when the focus of the poem shifts from Rādhā (the proper subject for a Vaiṣṇava lyric) to her confidante Bhānu (out of humility, the devotee ought never be the subject). From a Vaiṣṇava perspective, Tagore improperly mixes the devotional moods: servitude and humility, and even displays of awe and respect, sully the erotic. It is a shift that is consonant with Rabindranath's mature religious sensibility, one that seemed nearly fully formed by the time of *Gītāñjali, Gītimālya,* and *Gītālī*. Kṛṣṇa does not remain the cowherding cad of

14. Rabindranath Tagore, *My Reminiscences,* trans. Surendranath Tagore (London: The Macmillan Company, 1917), p. 138.

Braj, but seems to be recognized as the Lord, immanent in all creation, and in the hearts of his devotees. One is reminded of Rabindranath's attitude of reverence and submission to his *jīvan devatā,* his indwelling lord.

At these moments the reader is invited to follow the narrative into allegory, Rādhā and the *gopīs* but personifications of the soul longing for union with an elusive God. The move is familiar in mystical circles, reminiscent of Rumi, Meister Eckhart, and Donne. Read this way, Rabindranath's Bhānusiṃha poetry becomes what much of his poetry is understood to be, especially in the West: a culturally rooted statement of the more universal experiences of mystical union and separation. The allegorical interpretation blunts any suggestion that these poems could be construed as literally autobiographical; that is, in the sense of young Rabindranath desperately in love with his Kadambari. Though Rabindranath claimed in his memoirs that the songs were not Vaiṣṇava, the Vaiṣṇava assumption that the poetry must reveal the true nature of the author's personal experience of love might ironically prove to be right: the poetry reveals a spiritual bent that is unmistakably Tagore's. And nowhere can this be seen more than in Rabindranath's romanticizing and personification of death, and his longing for the release that death promises.

Death is a topic that is atypical of Vaiṣṇava poetry. But the Bhānu poems are arranged in a sequence that ends with Bhānu and Rādhā both growing old, looking back on what was and what might have been. Death certainly enters the drama at the point when life is spent but unfulfilled, Death alone seeming to offer a much-anticipated prospect of the Lord's embrace. This desire of achieving liberation through death permeates *Gitanjali* and much of his last poems. The sensibility and imagery at the end of the Bhānu cycle is very reminiscent of his talk with Death-as-the-groom in *Gītāñjali* (song 116), translated and heavily edited by Tagore in the English edition (song 91):

O thou the last fulfilment of life, Death, my death, come
and whisper to me!
Day after day have I kept watch for thee; for thee have I
borne the joys and pangs of life.
All that I am, that I have, that I hope and all my love have
ever flowed towards thee in depth of secrecy. One final
glance from thine eyes and my life will be ever thine
own.
The flowers have been woven and the garland is ready for
the bridegroom. After the wedding the bride shall leave
her home and meet her lord alone in the solitude of
night.

This same wistful yearning and resignation that closed the cycle of Bhānu, seems to have closed his own life. On 27 July 1941, just eleven days before he died, he dictated the following poem, which, recalling his indwelling Lord, seems to echo Bhānu's probing query in poem 20: "Who are You, who keeps my heart awake?" Like Bhānu and Rādhā, Rabindranath waited a lifetime for this tryst:

The sun of the first day
Put the question
To the new manifestation of life—
Who are you?
There was no answer.
Years passed by.
The last sun of the day
Uttered the question on the shore of the western sea,
In the hush of the evening—
Who are you!
No answer came.[15]

15. Trans. Dutta and Robinson in *Rabindranath Tagore: The Myriad-Minded Man*, p. 367; the original can be found in *Rabīndra Racanāvalī*, vol. 26, pp. 49–50.

Tagore's lifelong fascination with the Bhānu songs suggests that they were anything but juvenilia; they stand apart in his vast corpus as his most frequently revised works. The mythical setting of the songs is one familiar to any Bengali speaker, yet their content—especially the looming presence of death in the latter poems—violates the Vaiṣṇava expectations on which they depend. That interruption should give the reader pause, for it signals the works are more than the Vaiṣṇava songs they appear to be. Of a piece with Rabindranath's self-appointed search, they subtly explore the myriad complexities of human and divine love. In the end, this small set of songs yields a superfluity of interpretation, quietly probing what this great poet fervently believed was an uncommon, but universal, experience.

Appendix: The Life of Bhānusiṃha Ṭhākura[16]

It is impossible to determine in which precise years of the Christian era what idiots or sages were born or died to this world, and from this it can be concluded definitively that the land of India has no real history. On this matter the learned Hutchinson Saheb, in his seminal treatise, which has been grounded in the most enlightening research—and from which I quote—has opined, "If there is no factual history, we cannot know the first thing concerning times past."[17]

There has been, of course, no history at all in our country, and if there is no history, the real measure of the country cannot be ascertained. Lamentably nothing can be definitively determined about that crown-jewel of Vaiṣṇavas, the most ancient of poets,

16. In year 1291 of the Bengali Era (B.S.) — or A.D. 1884 — a short fictional biography of the now-infamous poet Bhānusiṃha appeared in the journal *Navajīvana*. Rabindranath was, of course, the author of the putative biography, which really makes it a humorous exercise in fictional autobiography. In keeping with his general disdain of the English education system, his biography was a parody of Western scholarship. This biography appeared replete with fictional footnotes in bad form, appropriately convoluted in their disclaimers, filled with specious references to exaggerated German titles, and even a spoof on the American Indian (not to be confused with the Indian Indian), whose footnoted reference — *The Grammar of the Red Indian Tchouk-Tchouk-Hmhm-Hmhm Language* — when pronounced in Bengali sounds the telltale clucking tongue and head-wagging hum of one who disapproves of something, or, with a slight change of intonation, the *tsk* of recognition by one who knows one has been had. The exaggerated and overly pedantic style has been preserved in the translation.
17. *Memoires of Cattermob Cruikshank Hutchinson*, vol. V, P. 1058. If there are any mistakes in spelling or orthography of the Englesh, the readers will understand that they are the fault of the printer. During the one and one-half years I studied Englesh with Bhabānī Master, I was not allowed to read any Bengali, so these mistakes will have sprouted of their own accord like so many thorni bushes.

Bhānusiṃha Ṭhākura. This has been no minor source of misery for some time, so we have endeavored to wipe clean this smudge on the vanity-mirror of the Land of the Bhāratas. And it is our sincere hope that we have been successful in this. All that we have determined is the unexpurgated truth, facts about which there can be no doubt.

First we must calculate the time and date of Bhānusiṃha Ṭhākura's birth. Some say he lived before Vidyāpati, others say later. Well if he came before, just how much before? And if he came later, how much later? There are several authoritative books from which we can glean much helpful information. And so,

First. There are the four Vedas: *Ṛk, Yajus, Sāma,* and *Atharva.* Whether the Vedas are really three or four has not even been fully determined; well, we have firmly fixed it, but many others have not. It cannot be doubted that there are at least three among the Vedas. In the *Ṛg Veda* is written: "*ṛṣaya strayī vedā viduḥ ṛco yajuṃṣi sāmāni.*" Nor is it not unknown by many what is written in the *Śatapatha Brāhmaṇa* of the fourth. Those who have the leisure to pore over the *sūtras* of the Vedas will discover therein that the *Atharva Veda* has no beginning. And with that in mind, the evidence suggests that the books of the Veda number none other than three. Now let us look carefully at the evidence pertaining to Bhānusiṃha that can be divined from these three Vedas. In the Veda one finds *chanda* (metrics and prosody), one finds *mantra* (magical utterances), one finds *brāhmaṇa* (sacred knowledge), one finds *sūtra* (pithy philosophical statements), but of Bhānusiṃha nothing whatsoever is stated.[18] However, in the *saṃhitā* sections of the Vedas one finds stories of such deities as Indra, Varuṇa, Marut, Agni, Rudra, Rabi, etc., and yet by some inexplicable ignorance there are no references whatsoever to Bhānusiṃha in the historical writings.[19]

18. See *English Translation of Hitopadesha* by H. M. Dibdin, Vol. 3, Page 551.
19. Some exceptionally learned individuals have cast doubts about this connection, for among the various *ṭhākuras* (deities) mentioned, such as Indra and so forth, Rabi is understood to be an appropriate pseudonym for Bhānu, yet this is deemed highly unacceptable.

In the *Śrīmad Bhāgavata* and *Viṣṇu Purāṇa,* one finds stories of the royal line of Nanda. And there we find written the story that Mahāpadma Nandī would bring into the world eight sons, starting with Sumālya, so, too, we find the tales of the Brahmin Kauṭilya; yet in that same place we catch not the tiniest glimpse of reference to Bhānusiṃha.[20] Should a bold and confident writer assert that "Yes, one can find references to Bhānusiṃha there," and proceed to furnish incontrovertible proof, then he will have earned our and all of India's deepest gratitude and thanks.

An article on Bhoja was brought to our attention, and it contained an extended description of Bhoja's role as king, Lord of Dhara City. In it we found the following names of pandits: Kālidāsa, Karpūra, Kalīṅga, Kokila, and Śrīcandra. Even the names of Mucakunda, Mayūra, and Dāmodara could be located there, but the name of Bhānusiṃha was nowhere to be told.[21] Compare this quote from the *Viśvaguṇādarśa:*

> *māghaścoro mayūro murāri purasaro bhāravīḥ sāravidyaḥ /*
> *śrīharṣaḥ kālidāsaḥ kaviratha bhavabhūtyādayo bhojarājaḥ //*

Clearly Bhānusiṃha's name is not there.[22]

Thinking that Bhānusiṃha's name might be mentioned in Vikramāditya's Navaratna, we searched at length and saw:

> *dhanvantariḥ kṣapaṇakomara siṃha śaṅkurvetāla bhaṭṭa*
> *ghaṭakarpara kālidāsāḥ /*
> *khyātā varāha mihiro nṛpateḥ sabhāyāṃ ratnāni vai*
> *vararucirṇava vikramasya //*

Alas, Bhānusiṃha's name was not found there, either.[23] Still, some overly imaginative individuals suspect that Kālidāsa and

20. Vide *Pictorial Handbook of Modern Geography.* Vol. 1, Page 139.
21. See *Hon-chang-ching.* By kong-fu.
22. *Sāhanāmā,* second chapter.
23. Peterhoff's *Chromkroptologisheder Unterlutungeln.*

Bhānusiṃha will turn out to be one and the same. This wild speculation can be neither rejected nor ignored, because the two poets so closely resemble each other in their genius and in the power of their poetic craft.

Finally we found no mention of Bhānusiṃha anywhere, even though we have diligently investigated *Batriśasiṃhāsana* (*The Thirty-two Stories in Praise of the Lion-Throned Vikramaditya*), *Vetālapāciśa* (*Tales of the Twenty-five Vampires*), Tulsidāsa's *Rāmāyaṇa*, *The Arabian Nights*, and *Suśilāra Upākhyāna* (*The Story of the Good-Natured Boy*). So, let no one find fault with the nature of our inquiry—the fault lies with the books alone.

There are four prevailing views concerning the date of Bhānusiṃha's birth. The revered Pāñckari Bābu says that Bhānusiṃha's birth was prior to A.D. 451. The most distinguished and learned Sanātana Bābu says it was some time after 1689 of the Christian era. Nitāicaraṇa Bābu, chief of pandits revered throughout the universe, argues that Bhānusiṃha took birth some time between A.D. 1104 and 1799. And the great scholar Kālācā̃d De, recipient of the special favor of the Goddess of Learning herself, asserts that Bhānusiṃha was born either before the year A.D. 819 or after A.D. 1639, and about that he has no doubt whatsoever. In addition, there is a rumor spread among several of our dear friends and relatives to the effect that Bhānusiṃha, that "Sun Lion," illumined this world with his effulgence by taking birth in the Christian year of 1861. Our more intelligent readers will not have to be told just how untenable this proposition is. Be that as it may, we are promoting this as Bhānusiṃha's birth date of record. The most intellectually astute and discriminating readers will harbor no doubts regarding the incontrovertible nature of its truth.

In the eleventh chapter of the *Nīla Purāṇa*, Vaitasa Muni has been called Bhānava.[24] Thus can it be seen that he is born of the lineage of Bhānu. So, he came several generations after Bhānu, though it is difficult to pinpoint this precisely. Rāma is said to be

24. See *The Grammar of the Red Indian Tchouk-Tchouk-Hmhm-Hmhm Language*. Conjongation of Verbs. Vol. 3. Page 999.

Rāghava and Rāma was three generations after Raghu, so let us assume that Vaitasa was Bhānu's fourth generation. Calculating twenty years for each generation, then Vaitasa Muni's birthday should come more or less eighty years after the birth of Bhānusiṃha. Those who have read the *Rājātaraṅginī* know well that Vaitasa was a man of the year A.D. 518,[25] from which we can ascertain that Bhānusiṃha's birth was in the Christian year of 438. Yet were one to follow the evidence proffered by his use of language, Bhānusiṃha would be projected as even more ancient.

It is a common knowledge that the longer a language is spoken by a people, the more abbreviated it becomes. From the older Bengali "*gaman karilām*" comes "*gelum.*" From "*bhrātṛjāyā*" comes "*bhāj,*" from "*khullatāt,*" "*khuṛo.*" Can one find anywhere an example of longer words deriving from shorter? Therefore, Bhānusiṃha's "*pirīti*" is assuredly older than the word "*prīti,*" and "*tikhinī*" older the "*tīkṣna.*" In *Ṛg Veda* 18 can be seen "*tīkṣnāni sāyakāni,*" and everyone knows that the *Ṛg Veda* was composed before 4000 B.C. Now it takes a language about two thousand years to become ancient and change, so from this we can definitively conclude that Bhānusiṃha was born at least six thousand years before the Christian era. Therefore it has been proved beyond all doubt that Bhānusiṃha took birth on or about A.D. 438 or 6000 B.C. If anyone can refute this, we shall regard them as our dearest friend, for our goal is nothing other than to ascertain the truth, and toward that we have endeavored from the very opening of this essay through to its end.

There are other details of Bhānusiṃha's life that we have fixed, and so, if we can determine the place of his birth in the same fashion and degree of confidence, we shall rest easy. There are, of course, many different opinions on this matter. That great heel of respectability Sanātana Bābu says one thing, while the great devourer of things devotional, Rūpanārāyaṇa Bābu, says quite another. There is absolutely no need whatsoever to quote them

25. *History of the Art of Embroidery and Crewel Work.* Appendix.

here, because their opinions are untrustworthy, if not contemptible. And from what they have written it is clear that both authors have grown tails, hooves, and ears of some uncommon length. For those who have espoused their brand of history, let them first submit it to the standards of a proper school, then may they have the courage to counter my claims. I have publicly proclaimed, and without hesitation, that I bear not the slightest bit of malice toward those two writers, and should anyone refute me, I shan't be angry, but truly delighted, for I have fixed my vision on the general weal. And it is for the sake of that noble truth alone that I desire quite simply that their writings be burned by the *caṇḍālas*, the polluted handlers of corpses, and that their ashes be hurled into the waters of perdition, and the two authors be sealed in earthen pots and follow suit.

A stone slab has been found down in an old well at Trinkamalī on the island of Sri Lanka. And on this stone were located the first and last letters of Bhānusiṃha's name: a *bha* and a *ha*. The rest of the letters have been completely obliterated. Some argue that the *ha* is really the conjunct *kṣna,* while others say *ñjha,* but it is certainly a *ha*. Still some claim that the *bha* is really *rcca,* and another says *klai,* but if they were to consider it seriously, they would realize that there is no way for the above-mentioned characters to appear in the word *bhānusiṃha*. Therefore, we can conclude, Bhānusiṃha used to live in Trinkamalī; although it is still open to debate whether or not it was within the well.

And there is another pressing matter.

An image of the sun god, Sūrya, of which Bhānu is an alternate form, has been unearthed on a mountain in Nepal in an area near Katmandu; although an extensive search of the adjacent region produced no similar image of a *siṃha* or lion. During the time of occupation by the vile and foreign Muslims, so many of our books, so much of our history, so many temples, were indiscriminately destroyed, and so it is entirely possible that during this same time at the order of Aurangzeb this image of Siṃha the Lion may have been plundered. But recently in Peshawar, a farmer plowing his fields unearthed a carved head of Siṃha the Lion, and it was clear that this was the remaining section of the Nepalese Bhānu image. Nevertheless, its real meaning is of no great import, but from it we can deduce—in fact it is wholly probable and comes as no surprise—that Bhānusiṃha made his home in Nepal. But only the reader can judge whether he used to traipse back and forth from Nepal to Peshawar for work. And it wouldn't be at all surprising that he would go to the well in Trinkamalī from time to time, in order to bathe. But with respect to Bhānusiṃha's homeland, it would seem that the arguments of Aprakāśacandra Bābu, he of unerring intellect and hairsplitting acumen, are little more than the ravings of lunacy. He has publicly revealed that one side of a manuscript written in Bhānusiṃha's own hand bears the name of the city of Calcutta. The veracity of this we certainly do not accept. We are clearly able to prove that in the matter of Bhānusiṃha's reputed homeland, nothing but confusion has reigned. Bhānusiṃha has written unmistakably, "I reside in Calcutta" (others might say "I reside in Calcutta under a banyan tree"). But if this be true, has anyone found in Calcutta's many wells a similar stone slab containing equivalent irrefutable proof? According to the rules that govern language, it is entirely feasible for the word "Calcutta" to be written in the Apabhraṃśa of either Katmandu or Trinkamalī. And with that we can conclude that it was Bhānusiṃha himself who was confused regarding the precise whereabouts of his own dwelling.

Little about the life of Bhānusiṃha is known without caveat. Perhaps some other opinionated writers are able to divine it, but this writer humbly submits that he is totally ignorant on the matter. And about his vocation, some have figured that he was a woodcutter with a small shop, while others claim he was a priest, a *pūjārī,* of the Lord of the Universe, God.

About Bhānusiṃha's poetry, however, I cannot say enough. It is material stolen from Mother Sarasvatī, the Goddess of Wisdom herself. It is rumored that this poetry used to reside in heaven, hidden in Sarasvatī's own stringed *vīṇā.* Once when it came within the range of Viṣṇu's ear, he realized that a second hearing would melt his heart beyond recovery, and so, fearing that, the personal attendants of Lakṣmī, the Goddess of Prosperity, stole it away and spirited it down to the world of mortality, where it was vouchsafed in Bhānusiṃha's brilliant mind. Many have said that his poetry is written in a fashion after Vidyāpati, but that only elicits laughter. No one has tried to discover if he does or doesn't have anything in common with Vidyāpati.

And with that, all the particulars of Bhānusiṃha's life that can be, have been irrefutably ascertained. Then again, this Bhānusiṃha just may not even be a Vaiṣṇava poet, but who can tell? Whether he is or isn't ultimately is a trifling matter—and *that* more than any other issue has been determined to be the *bona fide* truth.

Nabajīvana (Śrāvana, 1291 B.S. [1884])

About the Translators

TONY K. STEWART is a Bengali language and area specialist whose research and teaching focus on the religious literatures of the fourteenth through nineteenth centuries. Trained at The University of Chicago, his research on the Hindu Vaiṣṇava traditions of Bengal led him to specialize in the Brajabuli literary dialect of Bengali. Supported by fellowships from the National Endowment for the Humanities, the U.S. Department of Education's Fulbright-Hays program, the American Institute of Indian Studies, and the American Institue of Bangladesh Studies, he has worked extensively on the transcription and translation of unpublished handwritten Bengali manuscripts housed in Kolkata, India, and Dhaka, Bangladesh. Currently Stewart is Professor of South Asia religions at North Carolina State University, and Director of the North Carolina Center for South Asia Studies. He divides his time between Raleigh, Charleston, London, and Dhaka.

CHASE TWICHELL was born in New Haven, Connecticut, in 1950. She is the author of five books of poetry, including *The Snow Watcher* (Ontario Review Press, 1998), *The Ghost of Eden* (Ontario Review Press, 1995), and *Perdido* (Farrar, Straus & Giroux, 1991). She has won awards from the Artists Foundation (Boston), the New Jersey State Council on the Arts, and the American Academy of Arts and Letters, and fellowships from the Guggenheim Foundation and the National Endowment for the Arts. In 1999, Twichell quit teaching (at Princeton University) to start Ausable Press, which publishes contemporary poetry. She lives in Keene, New York, with her husband, the novelist Russell Banks.

Copper Canyon Press wishes to acknowledge the support of Lannan Foundation in funding the publication and distribution of exceptional literary works.

LANNAN LITERARY SELECTIONS 2003

James Galvin, *X: Poems*

Antonio Machado, *Border of a Dream: Selected Poems,*
translated by Willis Barnstone

Antonio Porchia, *Voices,* translated by W. S. Merwin

Rabindranath Tagore, *The Lover of God,*
translated by Tony K. Stewart and Chase Twichell

César Vallejo, *The Black Heralds,* translated by Rebecca Seiferle

LANNAN LITERARY SELECTIONS 2002

Cesare Pavese, *Disaffections: Complete Poems 1930–1950,*
translated by Geoffrey Brock

Kenneth Rexroth, *The Complete Poems of Kenneth Rexroth,*
edited by Sam Hamill and Bradford Morrow

Alberto Ríos, *The Smallest Muscle in the Human Body*

Ruth Stone, *In the Next Galaxy*

C. D. Wright, *Steal Away: Selected and New Poems*

LANNAN LITERARY SELECTIONS 2001

Hayden Carruth, *Doctor Jazz*

Norman Dubie, *The Mercy Seat: Collected & New Poems, 1967–2001*

Theodore Roethke, *On Poetry & Craft*

Ann Stanford, *Holding Our Own: The Selected Poems of Ann Stanford,*
edited by Maxine Scates and David Trinidad

Reversible Monuments: Contemporary Mexican Poetry,
edited by Mónica de la Torre and Michael Wiegers

LANNAN LITERARY SELECTIONS 2000

John Balaban, *Spring Essence: The Poetry of Hồ Xuân Hương*

Sascha Feinstein, *Misterioso*

Jim Harrison, *The Shape of the Journey: New and Collected Poems*

Maxine Kumin, *Always Beginning: Essays on a Life in Poetry*

W. S. Merwin, *The First Four Books of Poems*

The Chinese character for poetry is made up of two parts: "word" and "temple." It also serves as pressmark for Copper Canyon Press.

Founded in 1972, Copper Canyon Press remains dedicated to publishing poetry exclusively, from Nobel laureates to new and emerging authors. The Press thrives with the generous patronage of readers, writers, booksellers, librarians, teachers, students, and funders — everyone who shares the conviction that poetry invigorates the language and sharpens our appreciation of the world.

PGA *foundations*

THE ALLEN FOUNDATION *for* THE ARTS

Lannan

NATIONAL ENDOWMENT FOR THE ARTS

PUBLISHERS' CIRCLE

The Allen Foundation for The Arts
Lannan Foundation
National Endowment for the Arts

EDITORS' CIRCLE

The Breneman Jaech Foundation
Cynthia Hartwig and Tom Booster
Emily Warn and Daj Oberg
Washington State Arts Commission

For information and catalogs:

COPPER CANYON PRESS
Post Office Box 271
Port Townsend, Washington 98368
360/385-4925
www.coppercanyonpress.org

Set in Scala. The Bengali typeface is Barisal, designed by Clinton B. Seely. Book design and composition by Valerie Brewster, Scribe Typography. Additional composition by Cody Gates and Maureen Forys, Happenstance Type-O-Rama. Printed on archival-quality paper at Malloy, Inc.